LIGHT FROM THE DUST

A Photographic Exploration into the Ancient World of the Book of Mormon

SCOT FACER PROCTOR
MAURINE JENSEN PROCTOR

Designed by Kent Ware

Deseret Book Company
Salt Lake City, Utah

Library of Congress Catalog Card Number 93-72676
ISBN 0-87579-680-X (trade edition)
ISBN 0-87579-802-0 (limited edition)

Printed in the United States of America

10 9 8 7 6 5 4 3 2 1

CONTENTS

PERSONAL NOTES

We come with an agenda in this book. We love the Book of Mormon with all our souls, declare it boldly as holy scripture, and concur with the prophets that it is "the most correct of any book on earth, and the keystone of our religion."[1] Our deepest desire, "notwithstanding our weakness," is to proclaim that love in this, the last of the "trilogy of light" series.

Trying to capture on film what the Book of Mormon setting might have been like presented some challenges. Where do you go to shoot Zarahemla when no signs have yet been been found saying "Zarahemla —City Limits"? How can you document the Sidon when no river by that name exists on modern maps? How do you follow the path of Lehi from Jerusalem to Bountiful when the literal sands have blown over the trail for twenty-six centuries?

Clues overflow from the Book of Mormon itself. We once followed Hugh Nibley all over the Brigham Young University campus trying to get him to answer some questions on the Book of Mormon. His answers were terse. "It's in there. It's in there. It's in there," he said to nearly every question. Wonderfully, the wise and seasoned doctor was right. The answers are in the book itself.

During the 1980s, Australian Church members Warren and Michaela Aston conducted extensive research on all the candidates for Bountiful, where Nephi built his ship. Searching the coastline of the Arabian Peninsula, using Nephi's description as a standard, they narrowed the possibilities to just a few sites, then, finally, to a beach in Oman, near the border of Yemen, named Wadi Sayq (pronounced "sike"). Wadi Sayq has "much fruit," a mountain nearby where Nephi could go "oft and pray oft," hardwood trees for shipbuilding, flint for making fire, a freshwater source, and evidence of former human habitation. It is the only place yet located that entirely fits Nephi's description. So in 1992, with only the Astons' hand-sketched maps and descriptions, we headed for this remote spot.

At the village nearest Wadi Sayq, we were told the only way in to the wadi was by ship. No known trails or roads could lead us into the beach surrounded on both seaward sides by steep cliffs. In the evening darkness, we drove out of the village and parked by the beach, trying to find a place to rest. The stars shone brightly over the Arabian Sea, the northeastern curve of the Indian Ocean.

As we walked along the breaking waters, a pair of headlights came our way accompanied by an insistent honking. Nervous, we made our way back to the Jeep. Gathered to greet us were four natives, cold drinks in hand to welcome us to their village. They spoke Arabic; we spoke English. But somehow, by drawing in the sand and showing them our black-and-white photos of the wadi, we struck an agreement with them. The next day, a fourteen-year-old boy would take us the ten kilometers by boat.

Placing six thousand dollars' worth of camera

4

Afternoon light dapples some of the ruins of Quirigua (c. A.D. 300 to 900), located in eastern Guatemala near the border of Honduras. John Lloyd Stephens visited this and other cities just eleven years after the Book of Mormon was published and excited the mind of Joseph Smith, influencing him to publish, as editor of the Times and Seasons, the following: "It would not be a bad plan to compare Mr. Stephens' ruined cities with those in the Book of Mormon. Light cleaves to light and facts are supported by facts. The truth injures no one."[1] It is notable that Joseph's thinking on the geography of the Book of Mormon leaned to Central America, not South America as long tradition has held.

equipment into an eighteen-foot fishing boat was a little disquieting. The seven-foot waves crashing onto the beach looked as if they would easily swallow a Pentax, a Nikon, and us—and no life jackets were available. But this boy knew the ocean, he and his friend watched the waves, and at the signal they pushed us quickly bow first into the sea. Within minutes, at full throttle, we arrived at one of the most beautiful locations in the million square miles of Arabia. Wading through the night's tidewater pool, we brought our gear to a higher area and began drawing pictures in the sand to encourage the boy to to pick us up the next day. We would have thirty-two hours to photograph this place.

Wadi Sayq is one of two "rivers" in Arabia that flows with water all year round. Dolphins frolic at its outlet; flamingos search for food. We scouted for pictures in the early light, quickly realizing that we were there in the driest month of the year—May. This worked both to our advantage and to our disadvantage. The vegetation was not as beautiful for photography, but the indications of former habitation were more evident than they would have been if choked with undergrowth.

The report we used spoke only of a large mound, double lines of stones connected to the mound, and ancient graffiti on a cliff near the mound. Yet we began to see so much more. As we explored the side of the beach opposite from the mound, we saw hundreds of feet of double lines of stones, omega-shaped two-foot-high stone structures, a large retaining wall, a grave, and an ancient well. Who had built these in a place so much like that Nephi described?

While at Wadi Sayq we had prayed that the Lord would make known to us what happened here, if this indeed was the place where Nephi built the ship. We prayed to understand all we had seen. In the last few minutes we were there, we looked out from under our shade and felt the Spirit's impression, "Look!" We opened our eyes, and there, in a path we had walked over blindly perhaps five or six times, was a rock outline in the shape of a ship. How could we have missed it before? We walked around the outline, noting carefully the large buildup of rocks at the two ends and in the middle. We also noted the piles of rocks leading to the high-water tide line of the ocean, perhaps used as supports for a launching ramp.

Then we noted a large, concave, half-moon-shaped rock that could easily have been used with a bellows, because an air shaft ran underneath the rock. Noting the traces of carbon on the rock face, we wondered if this might have been like the foundry Nephi used, if not the very one. The ship outline was 130 feet long and 65 feet wide at the center, with the ends coming into points.

Miracles continued to follow us to Central America. One of the greatest miracles was the addition to our expedition of Dr. F. Richard Hauck, an archaeologist from Bountiful, Utah. Rick has spent his adult life in rigorous, on-site studies of possible Book of Mormon lands and is a spiritual, insightful, and choice man. Through his careful analysis, on-site reconnaissance, and thorough studies of the internal geographical clues of the Book of Mormon, Rick has been able to draw some significant corollaries with specific places in the Book of Mormon. We passed range after range of mountains, and Rick would nearly always say, "I've reconned that whole area twenty miles in every direction." Three of our six weeks in Central America were spent with him, and certainly much of what we photographed that is remarkable reflects his original research.

We leave with one last note about coming to the proposed land of Cumorah in southern Mexico. We hiked carefully through this area, tramping roads with mud up to our knees, braving rain and windstorms, climbing up mountains. We knew that Mormon, with four years to prepare for battle, would have fortified the site. Rick showed us a large basin filled with ancient, man-made fortifications, but none of us realized how extensive they were until we climbed a grassy man-made hill, itself of ancient origin, and saw the entire vista.

To the edge of the basin, in every direction, as far as we could see, were fortifications. Clearly, if this was not the site of the last struggle of the Nephites and Jaredites, it was the scene of an ancient battle of massive proportions that dates to the same periods. Never have we been so moved by any place in our travels as at this site in the Tuxtla (pronounced "tooshla") Mountains. Whether or not this was the site of the last struggles of the Nephites and of the Jaredites, we could feel the silent cries of millions who died here. If Mormon and Moroni fortified their people against the Lamanite attack in any fashion like that we saw in this basin, their love and desire to protect them— however hopeless—was more than we had ever supposed. We thought on Mormon's words to Moroni, "My beloved son, notwithstanding their hardness, let us labor diligently." So they had.

We are deeply indebted to Rick Hauck and his dear wife, Laura, for their sacrifices made to bring this book about. Our hearts are full of gratitude for our beloved friends, Elder John and Sister Diane Madsen, who were a stopover refuge for us in Monterey, Mexico, and a constant source of support and love. Our dear neighbors, Grant and Amie Cannon, not only joined us for two weeks of our Central American journey but also supported us day after day with treats, meals, surprises, and love. We are deeply indebted to Scot's parents, Paul and Martha Proctor, who bravely moved into our home and took over our large family for the six weeks of our Central American tour. A standing ovation would be appropriate. Maurine's mother, Maurine Jensen, has been a constant source of love and support, with silent prayers filling our days with blessings. We are grateful to Bruce and Janet Brower of Guatemala City, who freely let us move into their home and establish a base of operations for nearly two weeks of our shooting. Thanks to our sister Rosemary and her husband, Kent, for their support, encouragement, and love. Thanks to our brother Lane, who is always, always there for us. Our son, Eliot, came with us on the Central American tour. He happily carried camera gear, packs, and tripod anywhere (all at the same time) so that we might obtain just the right picture. As always, we are deeply indebted to our friends at Deseret Book, specifically Ron Millett, Sheri Dew, Kent Ware, Jack Lyon, Patricia J. Parkinson, and Emily Watts.

We add this book to the increasing avalanche of books on the marvelous Book of Mormon, partially in response to the call of the prophet, Ezra Taft Benson. We pray that seeing the physical scenes reminiscent of the Nephites will spark your interest, excite your intellect, and touch your spirit.

PROLOGUE

The Book of Mormon is the record of not one but two ancient civilizations that flourished in the Americas and then collapsed through their own moral decay. It is as if by saying it twice, the recorders want to make their point absolutely clear to us, for whom they wrote it. Any people who follow their course will meet their end. The sad story of the Nephites and the Jaredites proves again historian Will Durrant's observation, "A great civilization is not conquered from without until it has destroyed itself within."[1] Thus, if the world the Book of Mormon describes sounds familiar, echoed in our own time, it should. Where does the downward spiral begin? When the people reject Jesus Christ and his laws.

Yet the plunge is not irreversible. Moroni, the last Nephite historian, seeing his civilization decimated, buried their record in a hill in upstate New York, then returned as an angel in 1827 to give this treasure to Joseph Smith. The record would come forth as a witness and warning to the latter-day world. These are ancient voices crying to us from the dust, pleading that we must learn from their people's folly and teaching what their prophets knew of Jesus Christ.

Yet it is tempting to look at the people presented in the book not as flesh and blood who actually lived, ate, dwelt in houses, and were finally buried somewhere but rather as vague ghosts who lived in nowhere land. In this we do them a disservice, for the message they would give us comes with the urgency and passion of real people. It is to cast them against their backdrop and fill in the blank corners of our imagination that this book has been created.

They lived somewhere, but where? Which piece of pottery, which unexcavated mound is theirs? Not Joseph Smith nor any other Church leader has shared revelation or given us a definitive answer on these questions. Most of the original geographical ideas on the matter seem to be merely a reflection of early leaders' best thinking, given the evidence available.

Entire traditions have followed. An 1836 record in Frederick G. Williams's handwriting stated that Lehi landed "in South America, in Chile, thirty degrees, south latitude."[2] This information was originally attributed to Joseph Smith, but Williams later claimed that an angel gave it to him. Scholars John A. Widtsoe and B. H. Roberts were skeptical of its origin. In the late 1800s Orson Pratt's idea was widely embraced. He held that the land northward was North America, the land southward was South America, and the narrow neck of land was the isthmus of Panama. Mostly because of Pratt's philosophy, the Book of Mormon from 1876 to 1920 had specific, modern geographical descriptions in the footnotes. Yet, studying the internal evidence of the Book of Mormon, B. H. Roberts wrote, "There is no evidence . . . that warrants such a conclusion."[3] Such vast distances were not described in the text.

Beyond a few exceptions such as these, Church

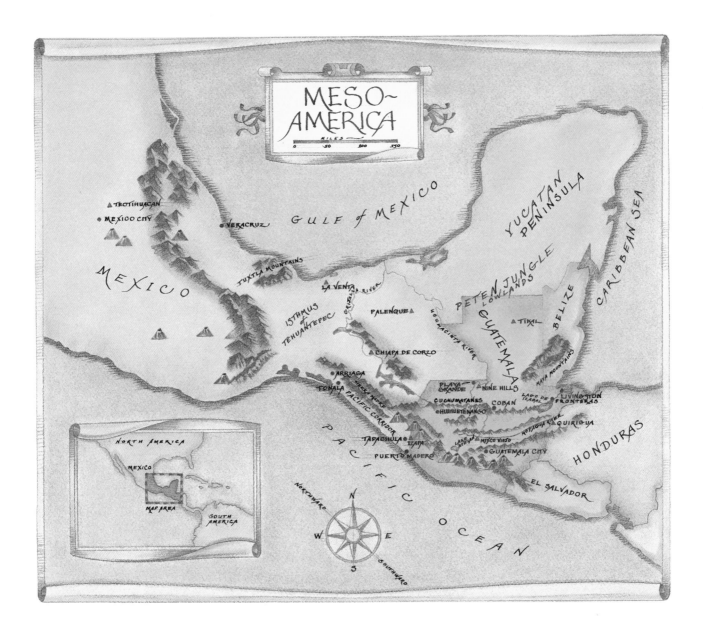

leaders have been careful to avoid tying the Book of Mormon to a specific location, because testimony of the book's truth should stand not on outward evidences but on the witness of the Holy Ghost. We cannot, then, draw a map based on authority. The Lord has not revealed the locations of the action of the Book of Mormon; He has left us to piece together the puzzle the best we can.

That invitation is open to us. In 1841 a book entitled *Incidents of Travel in Central America, Chiapas, and Yucatan* was published, presenting to the world a picture of the ancient cities of Mesoamerica as seen by John Lloyd Stephens and artist Frederick Catherwood. Opening the door on this unknown world swept the nation with excitement. Extracts of the book were printed in the September 1842 issue of *Times and Seasons,* then under the editorial direction of Joseph Smith, and further comment was made in the October issue. The newspaper stated, "It would not be a bad plan to compare Mr. Stephens' ruined cities with those in the Book of Mormon. Light cleaves to light and facts are supported by facts. The truth injures no one."[4]

During Joseph Smith's time and in a newspaper he supervised, then, we are pointed to southern Mexico and Guatemala as the possible Book of Mormon lands, but recent scholarship has centered there for many more reasons. First, the Book of Mormon gives us a clear, consistent picture of the location of its landmarks. We learn, for instance, of a land southward and a land northward separated by a narrow neck of land. The land southward is divided into the land of Nephi in the south, where the Lamanites live, and the land of Zarahemla in the north, where the Nephites live.

The land of Nephi is in the highlands; the land of Zarahemla in the lowlands. They are separated by a narrow strip of wilderness, perhaps a mountain range, that runs east and west. The entire land southward is nearly surrounded by seas. A major river they called the Sidon drains the area, running north. The west wilderness, again perhaps a mountain range, runs along the sea in the west. What area matches this rather specific description? Southern Mexico and Guatemala.

Mesoamerica becomes an even more likely candidate when its history is considered. Ninety percent of the ruins in the Americas that date to the appropriate time are found in this region. The people who lived here are the only people before the Europeans arrived who had a written language. Their civilization was marked by high cultural achievement in religion, architecture, agriculture, calendrics, and astronomy.

What's more, the history of the area reveals interesting comparisons to our Book of Mormon history. Anthropologists note that two traditions are evident here. The first tradition, the Olmecs, stretched from perhaps 2,500 B.C. to just after 600 B.C. New scholarship points to their having come from across the ocean. Their society was marked by periodic rises and declines and ended in an internal upheaval. When their strength as a society was destroyed, remnants of the people remained and markedly influenced the populations that followed, just as the Jaredites influenced the Nephites.

It is not easy to pinpoint the beginning of the second tradition, which is associated with the Maya, but clearly by 125 B.C., when King Benjamin ruled in the Book of Mormon, they were moving into a period of high civilization and growth. Near 75 B.C. "a rather sudden change occurred. People abandoned many of the scattered settlements and moved into major communities."[5] This is best explained by "the threat of war."[6]

In 73 B.C., of course, the war between the Nephites and Lamanites began that would stretch on for thirteen years. Then, the first century A.D. leaves a quiet archaeological record, what one researcher calls "a pause in their headlong course of development"[7] that seems to coincide with the simplicity and classlessness of a perfect society. At last, "the Second Tradition reached peak vigor between A.D. 250 and 300."[8] True to the Book of Mormon's description of apostasy, the society was marked by wealth and class distinction, elaborate building programs, and the predominance of a ceremonial religion. While the classic period (A.D. 200–900) was a time of cultural flourishing when many ancient Mesoamerican temples were built, it was also a time of warfare and rivalries.

While this description is a only a broad sweep, the conditions described in the Book of Mormon clearly fit its pattern. Still, we are left with a multiplicity of questions. For instance, we see many cultural groups in Mesoamerica, not just two, and studying the area leads one to the conclusion that the Book of Mormon is the record of two lineage groups, the Nephites and Jaredites, and not the history of all the Indians. If we were to write the history of the Mormon people, it would not be the history of the United States. We would write what was important to us. This may be the case with the Nephites. What happened to them is only a fraction of what happened during the same period in Mesoamerica.

What's more, the Lord decreed that if they did not serve Him, he would sweep them from the earth. In southern Mexico and Guatemala, one sees thousands of ancient mounds and walls, the remains of forgotten cities, many tangled in jungle growth. Other remains are buried under lava flows, hidden in lakes, buried under centuries of earth. Even while scholars of every persuasion work to solve the riddle of Mesoamerica, it remains one of the great mysteries of the world. It is easier to tell when a particular piece of pottery was used than to know who the people were who used it, where they came from, or why they disappeared.

Until evidence is found to pinpoint a particular location, we will have to talk about Book of Mormon locations in tentative terms. Still, it is remarkable to read of Captain Moroni's trenches and find an area today that corresponds to the description of Manti, lined with miles of such trenches. It is moving to be in the Tuxtla Mountains, a possible candidate for Cumorah, and see a basin filled with ancient fortifications where a massive battle was clearly fought.

Yes, but what are we to make of the Hill Cumorah in New York where Joseph Smith clearly found the plates? Isn't this the same Hill Cumorah where the last battle was fought? Many students of the Book of Mormon no longer think so, assuming there may be two Cumorahs, one in Central America and one in New York where Moroni, after thirty-six years of wandering, finally buried the plates.

If the Book of Mormon lands *are* in Mesoamerica, it is highly unlikely that Limhi's group, who were "many days"[9] trying to find Zarahemla, would have wandered thousands of miles, across major land barriers, and not known they had missed the mark long before they found the land "covered with the bones of men"[10] if it were in New York.

Those who favor a New York Cumorah as the last battle scene usually point to two pieces of evidence. The first is an experience Joseph Smith and Oliver Cowdery had of seeing the Hill Cumorah open to reveal a room full of plates. Heber C. Kimball specifically called this experience a "vision,"[11] thus it could easily have been a different Cumorah than the one in New York.

The second piece of evidence is an experience during Zion's Camp when Joseph and the men found some bones of a man Joseph identified as Zelph, a Lamanite. Willard Richards wrote the account that appeared in the 1934 and 1948 editions of the *History of the Church* as if he were Joseph, referring to a prophet Onandagus who was known "from the hill Cumorah or eastern Sea, to the Rocky Mountains."[12] Yet Joseph apparently edited out the Hill Cumorah reference, and it is his edited version that appears in the 1904 edition of the *History of the Church*. Those who would use this reference, then, to point to New York as the scene of the last battle are on inconclusive grounds.

Wherever the events of the Book of Mormon took place, its message is certain. It is another testament of Jesus Christ, a missive of love from the Lord, to teach us his mission and attributes in a world that has forgotten them.

1 LET US BE STRONG LIKE UNTO MOSES

Pages 12–13: Light penetrates clouds of an ominous afternoon sky in modern-day Yemen, where the ancient frankincense trail turned eastward and where Lehi and his family may have been camping when Ishmael died. Nahom was the only place in the wilderness journey that the record indicates was already named when the party arrived.

Above: The "land of Jerusalem" took in a much larger area than the city Jerusalem, including this place a few miles to the south at Bethlehem. Lehi speaks in similar words to the Prophet Joseph Smith describing his vision as "a pillar of fire."[1] Though both prophets were persecuted for saying they had seen a light, neither could deny it.

In 600 B.C., Jerusalem was flourishing, her bazaars laden with precious things from the farthest reaches of the ancient world, her citizens prosperous. Who could foresee that it would all suddenly vanish in smoke? One group. Into this world of illusive security came many prophets with a gloomy message. Jeremiah, Ezekiel, Nahum, Habukkuk, Zephaniah, Zechariah, and one Lehi spoke with the same unrelenting words of doom—unless Jerusalem repented of her idolatry, dishonesty, and corruption, she would be destroyed. Poised strategically on the path between two rival world powers, Egypt and Babylonia, Jerusalem was, indeed, in a precarious position. She had been a vassal of both Egypt and Babylonia, and parties supporting both sides existed side by side in the land, each accusing the other of bad judgment. In this divided city, the prophets' words sounded like defeatism, negativism, treason. The corrupt elders demanded that they be imprisoned and executed for destroying the morale of the people. Passions ran high when ill-fated King Zedekiah chose to suicidally ally with Egypt.

Flock of young lambs huddle together in fold near Jerusalem on April 6. In keeping with the exacting patterns of the Lord, could Lehi and his family have left Jerusalem on this specific date, six hundred years before the coming of the Savior?

15

When a society is ripe for destruction, the Lord's pattern is to save the righteous by removing them to a place of refuge. In spiritual history, that place has been the wilderness, idealized by Israel as the place to commune with God. So it would be for Lehi, whose preaching was met with such a violent reaction that the Lord warned him in a dream to take his family and steal away into the desert south of Jerusalem. He voiced no objections, nor did he ask how to prepare for the journey. Evidence suggests that he had been a bold, resourceful merchant who already knew the ways of the scorching desert, a citizen of the world who had forged new markets, cultivated foreign contacts, was deeply aware of Egyptian culture. He had given his youngest sons, Nephi and Sam, Egyptian names, and had taught them to write in reformed Egyptian. He had established a great fortune and belonged to Manasseh, which of all tribes lived the farthest out in the desert.[2] Not surprisingly, the Lord had fashioned Lehi's life to perfectly prepare him for what lay ahead.

Down past the treeless reaches of the Dead Sea, Lehi took his wife, Sariah, and sons, Laman, Lemuel, Sam, and Nephi, being directed toward a promised land where they could create a colony based on higher moral standards and purer traditions than apostate Jerusalem. Yet the little group already harbored the seeds of their ultimate destruction. Laman and Lemuel "knew not the dealings of that God who had created them"[3] and thought their father's visions to be "the foolish imaginations of his heart."[4] Blind materialists to the bone, they did not believe Jerusalem could be destroyed. They lived for short-term satisfaction, grabbed for power, and whined without hope for the loss of their fortunes. Not knowing God, they could not trust His word, and their wilderness journey would be all heat and thirst and no purpose.

Their younger brother Nephi, however, had "great desires to know of the mysteries of God"[5] and cried unto the Lord until He visited Nephi. It was not attitude or good cheer that would make Nephi's journey ahead so different from that of his brothers, but rather knowing the Lord.

Having safely separated themselves by perhaps several hundred miles from the murderous threats of Jerusalem, Lehi's sons were now commanded by the Lord to return to the city and obtain the plates of brass from their keeper, Laban. These were the sacred records of the Jews from the beginning and critical to preserving their language and understanding of God for their posterity in a new land.

Twelve to fifteen days would have been needed to traverse the rugged desert of the Negev, span the scorching heat of Wadi Al Araba, and climb "up" the final four thousand vertical feet to Jerusalem. The Book of Mormon is consistent in the use of the words "up" and "down," which always refer to changes in elevation.

Nephi's description of Laban, a powerful leader in Jerusalem, is a thumbnail sketch of the city's utter decadence. He is a military type, perhaps a commander of fifty, very large, quick-tempered, lustful, unscrupulous, a cruel bargainer, and given to drink—and it is his type who is in control of the city. The gravity and danger of their mission is emphasized in Laman's first encounter with the man. He asked for the plates, and Laban exploded in anger, calling him a robber. "I will slay thee,"[9] he yelled as Laman fled away. The brothers would have given up at this point, but Nephi was certain that the Lord would provide a way for them to keep His commandments. Next, with Nephi's encouragement, they gathered up their own wealth, brought it to Laban, and offered to buy the plates. This time Laban sent his servants after them, and they fled again, narrowly escaping death and leaving their fortune behind.

To Laman and Lemuel, this was an impossible fool's mission, and in a cave in the wilderness, they beat their brothers with a rod until an angel came and stood before them, commanding, "Behold ye shall go up to Jerusalem again."[10] But even an angel could not help Laman and Lemuel, whose faith was strictly in the arm of flesh. The angel had just left when they turned again to their murmuring: "How is it possible that the Lord will deliver Laban into our hands? Behold, he is a mighty man, and he can command fifty, yea, even he can slay fifty; then why not us?"[11]

Pages 16–17: The ancient King's Highway in modern Jordan is a likely route for Lehi and his family to have traveled as they journeyed south. Lehi "was a man of three cultures, being educated not only in 'the learning of the Jews and the language of the Egyptians'[6] but in the ways of the desert as well."[7]

Above: Cavities in the rock like this one dot the limestone hills and valleys outside the city of Jerusalem. "One of the main functions of any governor [such as Laban] in the East has always been to hear petitions, and the established practice has ever been to rob the petitioners (or anyone else) wherever possible."[8]

Right: Ruins in this southeastern section of Jerusalem give physical evidence of the Babylonian destruction around 587 B.C. One house found here contained a jar of bullae, *the official seals of government. Perhaps this house is similar to the house of Laban, who may have lived in this area of the city.*

Darkness lay over the great city as Nephi's brothers hid without the walls and Nephi crept alone toward the house of Laban. With narrow streets and no lamps, the pathways would have been nearly devoid of light or shadow. "To move about late at night without lamp bearers and armed guards was to risk certain assault."[12] Twice the brothers had used their own devices to obtain the plates and twice failed, but now Nephi would be "led by the Spirit, not knowing beforehand the things which [he] should do."[13] Only with the Lord's aid could he find success.

Finding Laban prostrate and drunk in the street, decked in armor and sword, was a telltale sign of the deteriorated condition of Jerusalem. He had been meeting with the elders of the church under the cover of night, perhaps plotting ways to continue to deceive the people about the precarious state of the nation.

Here, unconscious before the large and powerful Nephi, was the keeper of the records, and the Spirit said that he should kill him. But Nephi said in his heart: "Never at any time have I shed the blood of man."[14] Repeatedly Nephi shrank from the promptings, but he was convinced when the Spirit said, "It is better that one man should perish than that a nation should dwindle and perish in unbelief."[15] Swiftly and without further hesitation, Nephi smote off Laban's head. The nation to be saved would be not only Nephi's but also our own.

Now Nephi moved boldly, quickly, putting on all of Laban's clothes, including the armor and sword, and headed to the treasury, where he met Laban's trusted servant Zoram, who had the keys. With the voice of Laban, Nephi commanded that Zoram get the plates and follow him. Outside the walls, trembling, Zoram realized his mistake and would have fled, but Nephi seized him and with the most powerful oath of Eastern culture, "as the Lord liveth, and as I live,"[16] calmed Zoram and promised his safety and freedom if he would follow them. Zoram immediately shifted allegiance to these strangers, and the Lord would raise up a branch to Zoram, too, in the promised land.

Pages 20–21: Nighttime exposure of the Kidron Valley on the east and south of the city Jerusalem. The brothers could have come up this way and easily secreted themselves in this ravine outside the walls of the city while Nephi crept in to find Laban. The sword of Laban became a sacred relic to the Nephites and would go at the forefront of their battles. When Joseph Smith last saw the sword of Laban, it was laid across the gold plates

unsheathed, "and on it was written these words: 'This sword will never be sheathed again until the kingdoms of this world become the kingdom of our God and his Christ.' "[17]

Above: Common food of the Bedouin since ancient times are these rock-hard Jamid, which are made from a mixture of herbs, meadow grasses, and camel's or goat's cheese. The mixture is placed in a

skin bag, then kneaded and dried on the tent roof in the hot sun. Concerning a teaching of Joseph Smith, Erastus Snow said that Ishmael's "sons married into Lehi's family."[18] Marrying cousins is a Near Eastern custom that survives to this day. It is poignant that Lehi and Sariah were anxious to bring Ishmael's family into the wilderness. Their own daughters would have been in that group.

Their sons had likely been absent over a month, and in their wilderness camp, Sariah mourned, "My sons are no more, and we perish in the wilderness."[19] Upon their return with the plates of brass, Sariah rejoiced, "Now I know of a surety that the Lord hath commanded my husband to flee into the wilderness."[20] She, like others, received her witness after the trial of her faith.

In Lehi's early searchings of the plates, he discovered that he was a descendant of Joseph, "who was sold into Egypt, and who was preserved by the hand of the Lord, that he might preserve . . . all his household from perishing."[21] Here was a profound type. Just as Joseph had been removed from Israel to save them from starvation, so his posterity had now been called away from Israel, that their record would come forth in the last days and save Israel again, this time starving for want of the word of God.

To preserve seed in the promised land, the Lord asked Lehi's sons to return again to Jerusalem, this time to bring back Ishmael and his family that they might take his daughters to wed.

Camels can carry loads of up to 1,000 pounds, go two or three weeks without water, and survive in scorching heat of 140 degrees Fahrenheit. So important are camels "there are a thousand Arabic terms for [them] in various stages of growth. They still supply the desert nomad with transport, food, and wealth. He drinks their milk, eats their flesh, weaves their hair into tents and cloaks, burns their dung for fuel, uses their urine for medicine and hair tonic, and uses the beast to turn his waterwheel and pull his plow."[22] The lack of mention of them in the record is not surprising, as they were the common means of transportation in the desert.

23

Above: A great and spacious building in the days of Lehi may have been like the palace of Bilquis, the Queen of Sheba, with towers reaching to a great height and windows throughout. Located in Marib, Yemen, this palace was the crossroads of the ancient capital of Sheba, one of the wealthiest cities in Arabia in Lehi's time. The poet Shelley described the decaying remains of a once-colossal desert sculpture, whose pedestal bore these words: "Look on my works, ye Mighty, and despair!" Wrote Shelley, "Nothing beside remains. Round the decay/Of that colossal wreck, boundless and bare/The lone and level sands stretch far away."[23]

Even as Joseph of Egypt, his forebear, Lehi was a dreamer.[24] Dreams and visions had shown him the impending destruction of Jerusalem and the coming of the Messiah. Obedience to the Lord's command in a dream led him away from his homeland. Now Lehi gathered the twenty-two or more people of the camp and told them of another transcendent dream that centered on the tree of life, an archetypal image so expressive of life's ultimate, spiritual meaning that it appears in many ancient cultures. Some scholars suggest that it is under a tree of life that Buddha sat; they say the Jewish menorah is another form of the tree.

The centerpiece of the dream is a tree of exceeding beauty "whose fruit was desirable to make one happy."[25] In this pivotal symbol of a tree converges all the meaning of the gospel. It was the tree of life that stood in the Garden of Eden and nourished Adam and Eve. This was a place of unity with each other and with the Lord. After they fell, eating the fruit of a forbidden tree, they came

24

into a world of duality, division, separation from God. The only way to be at-one again with the Lord comes from the events that took place on another tree—the cross, through Christ's atonement and resurrection. Some legends even claim the cross was constructed from a branch of the tree of life. Symbolically, at least, this is true. Finally, if we will plant the word of God in our heart and nourish it, it too "shall be a tree springing up unto everlasting life."[26]

When Lehi tasted of the fruit of the tree of life, "it filled [his] soul with exceedingly great joy."[27] In fact, his mortal words failed him, and he could not capture the overwhelming feelings of sweetness he had nor the understanding that was given to him. The tree of life was the love of God shed forth unto the children of men—it was a symbol of Jesus Christ. And "numberless concourses of people" were pressing forward, striving to "obtain the path which led unto the tree."[28]

Pages 26–27: The tremendous Dead Sea rift zone, of which this Wadi Al-Arabah gorge is part, extends through parts of Jordan and Israel and may have been similar to the "great and . . . terrible gulf"[29] that separated the righteous from the wicked in Lehi's dream. The Al-Arabah is the deepest rift on the face of the earth and plunges to over 1,300 feet below sea level at the Dead Sea. This fault is active and extends from East Africa northward to the Sea of Galilee. One of the branch faults of this zone is just a few miles east of Jerusalem.

25

The fruit of this tree of life was so delicious that Lehi didn't want to enjoy it alone but immediately looked for his family members to come and eat too. The symbol here was not just of salvation but of an entire family coming to eternal life. Lehi was anxious that not one be lost. It is significant, as each verse in the Book of Mormon is, that the story of this dream comes just after the gathering of "seeds of every kind"[30] for their journey. Now Lehi was striving to gather his own seed—his children and massive posterity yet unborn.

The images that came to Lehi as he stood by the tree in his dream are those of a man of the desert. He saw a river of water leading to the tree and looked to see its source, as a desert dweller would. Then, he saw that many of those who pressed toward the tree became lost in a mist of darkness. The wanderer in the desert can be overtaken by thick, low-lying, nearly inpenetrable mists that move rapidly through a region and blind all who would travel on. Lehi saw many in the dream dangerously close to the river of filthiness, and they "did press forward through the mist of darkness, clinging to the rod of iron . . . until they did . . . partake of the fruit of the tree."[31] Nephi explained that the rod of iron "was the word of God; and whoso would . . . hold fast unto it, they would never perish."[32]

On the other side of the river from the tree was "a great and spacious building . . . high above the earth . . . filled with people . . . in the attitude of mocking and pointing their fingers towards those who . . . were partaking of the fruit."[33] These are the very antithesis of Jesus Christ, and the kind of gulf that separates them from the righteous would have been a common sight in Lehi's desert.

In 1811, Joseph Smith, Sr., had a remarkably similar vision. While he partook of the glorious fruit of the tree, he said in his heart, "I cannot eat this alone, I must bring my wife and children, that they may partake with me."[34] In exultation he said of the fruit, "The more we ate the more we seemed to desire, until we even got down upon our knees and scooped it up, eating it by double handfuls."[35]

After Lehi recounted his dream to his family, Nephi wanted to "see, and hear, and know"[36] the things his father had experienced and, believing that "he that diligently seeketh shall find,"[37] he approached the Lord. In few other passages of scripture are the steps so clearly outlined for obtaining knowledge as we see in Nephi's approach: "After I had *desired* to know the things that my father had seen, and *believing* that the Lord was able to make them known unto me, as I sat *pondering* in mine heart I was caught away in the Spirit of the Lord."[38] Nephi was taken to "an exceedingly high mountain,"[39] where a marvelous type was shown. The Spirit of the Lord "in the form of a man . . . spake unto [Nephi] as a man speaketh with another"[40] and asked Nephi a wonderful and simple question: "What desirest thou?"[41] What do you want? Here was deity speaking to mortal, and it was Nephi's desires that took the forefront. What joyous light is given in this simple view! Is the Lord a loving parent who cares about our needs and questions? Are the things that we want important to Him? The patterns here and throughout the scriptures give the answer: a resounding yes!

Now a glorious series of visions burst upon Nephi's view, all of them in answer to his desire to "behold the things which [his] father saw."[42] One hundred thirty-one verses are given to us from Nephi's vision and seem to indicate that we have but an abridged version of what Lehi saw. To teach Nephi the meaning of the tree of life, he was shown Mary, "a virgin, most beautiful and fair above all other virgins,"[43] who would not be born for nearly another six centuries. Then she was carried away in the Spirit, and Nephi saw Mary bearing a child in her arms. "Behold the Lamb of God, yea, even the Son of the Eternal Father!"[44]

Nephi was asked, "Knowest thou the meaning of the tree which thy father saw?"[45] How could he now know the meaning of the tree by seeing this baby in the arms of a virgin, unless the beautiful tree with abundant fruit was the very quintessence of the Father's love in the giving of His Only Begotten Son to save the world.

As Nephi's vision expanded, he was shown in great detail the mortal life and mission of the Messiah, Jesus Christ. Fifty-five times in the record of the vision, the Lord is referred to as the Lamb of God, the lamb image emphasizing that "great and last sacrifice"[49] that was to come.

Every detail of Lehi's dream was shown to Nephi and its meanings explained. The rod to which people must hold fast is the "word of God,"[50] and Nephi was shown the Bible, the Book of Mormon, and then "other books"[51] that would come forth "by the power of the Lamb."[52] The "large and spacious building" was the "vain imaginations and the pride of the children of men,"[53] or as Joseph Smith, Sr., was told by his guide, "It is Babylon, it is Babylon and it must fall."[54] Nephi was shown the exodus pattern again as a type of the history of the earth. Israel, which would be scattered, would be gathered again in the last days to build Zion. After wandering centuries in the wilderness, she too would be restored to the promised land.

The Lord's expansive plan was further unfolded to Nephi. He saw a nation set up among the Gentiles in the promised land, including the coming forth of Christopher Columbus[55] and the Pilgrims and other early colonizers.[56] He saw Great Britain gathered against the Colonies and the outcome of the Revolutionary War.[57]

Finally, Nephi was shown the establishing of the kingdom of God and the going forth of the Saints of God in taking the gospel to all the earth. Then shall it be made known "to all kindreds, tongues, and people, that the Lamb of God is the Son of the Eternal Father, and the Savior of the world; and that all men must come unto him, or they cannot be saved."[58]

Significantly, Nephi wrote only a fraction of what he saw in the vision,[59] the pattern being the same for Mormon,[60] Moroni,[61] Joseph Smith,[62] and John.[63] Each prophet had a foreordained mission to reveal specific parts of the Lord's plan, and though Nephi was shown the history and scenes of the end of the world, he was commanded not to write them. That mission was for John the beloved apostle yet to be born. Nephi saw him and bore record of his name, but he could not write the things John would later reveal.[64]

Pages 28–29: View at sunset across the Gulf of Aqaba near the border of modern Saudi Arabia and Jordan. Lehi refers to such an area in the record as the "fountain of the Red Sea."[46] Perhaps the most overwhelming thing that Nephi saw in his vision was the annihilation of his own posterity due to their pride and succumbing to the temptations of the devil. "I was overcome because of my afflictions . . . because of the destruction of my people, for I had beheld their fall."[47] The fall of the Nephites after 1,000 years would serve as a warning to any other nation upon the promised land who would not serve Jesus Christ.[48]

Beautiful wood carving of Stela 5, a possible representation of the dream of the tree of life, discovered with 21 other stelae and 19 altars at Izapa in Southern Mexico. In one of the earliest studies of Stela 5, an archaeologist, M. Wells Jakeman, found 22 correspondences and 114 points of agreement between the Izapa carving and the written accounts of Nephi and Lehi's tree of life visions. The old man sitting on the left may represent Lehi. The jawbone located immediately behind his head may be a glyph represent-ing Lehi's name, standing for the Valley of Lehi where Samson slew a thousand Philistines. The headdress on the woman to his left "can be considered as actually a kind of name-glyph" very much like Egyptian representations of a queen or princess. The name Sariah means "Princess of Yahweh."[65] The person on the right with the parasol over his head reveals "a serpent projecting out from his forehead; behind the serpent is a human face with a plant rising about and leaves flowing from it down the young man's back . . . [this] essentially duplicates the representations of the ancient Egyptian grain god, Nepri or Nepi"[66] V. Garth Norman interprets the bird-masked personage to the left and above Nephi as representing Quetzalcoatl, who "is holding supposed fruit or medicine bags, and that with his bird beak, forward bag, and forward foot touching the tree, he undoubtedly controls and directs . . . a journey to the Tree of Life."[67]

Above: Trees are extremely rare in the regions of the wilderness where Lehi and his family traveled and are generally found only in or near wadis. A wadi is a dried riverbed or wash that may run with water only two or three days a year from spring rains. The caravans and desert travelers always followed the wadis because of their vegetation and grasses for their animals and the presence of water a little beneath the surface. Wadis can be as small as a few feet wide to 50 miles wide and were the superhighways of the ancient deserts.

Right: Ancient, hand-cut steps in a side canyon of Wadi Musa, in modern Jordan, where Petra is located. The ancient King's Highway, the route Lehi may have traveled, comes by the mouth of the wadi. Lehi may have traded with the Edomites in this area as they had developed the arts of agriculture, pottery, weaving, and metalworking. In its heyday, hundreds of years after Lehi, the city of Petra supported a population of about 30,000.

Nephi descended from the mountain—where he had been carried away in the Spirit and seen visions of the coming of the Lord and the future of the earth—to a tent where his brothers were fighting with each other because they did not understand their father's prophecies. After his own heavenly manifestation, Nephi asked a most natural question, "Have ye inquired of the Lord?"[68] He knew from the most intimate, firsthand experience from whom they could obtain answers—"Ask, and it shall be given unto you"[69]—but their reply was telling. "We have not; for the Lord maketh no such thing known unto us."[70] That paradigm itself sealed their doom, was the mental filter through which all their experience would flow. Believing that the Lord would make no such thing known to them, they wouldn't ask, wouldn't trouble themselves, and their belief became its own self-fulfilling prophecy. Nephi would climb the mountain; they would grovel in the tent.

Nephi's own understanding was quite different. He believed that "the Lord knoweth all things from the beginning"[71] and would answer the prayers of the faithful. All his actions flowed from that reality. Shortly after they reached the promised land, Nephi was asked to make a set of large plates on which to engrave an account of his people. Then in about 569 B.C., the Lord asked him to make a second set of small plates for the special purpose of keeping their revelations and prophecies. It might seem natural to complain about this second assignment. Plates were difficult to make, engraving upon them slow and tedious. Why, after all, make a second set covering the same time period? Without a murmur, Nephi said, "The Lord hath commanded me to make these plates for a wise purpose in him, which purpose I know not."[72]

Yet, more than two thousand years later as Joseph Smith was translating the Book of Mormon from reformed Egyptian into English, he began with Mormon's abridgment of the large plates. He had translated 116 pages when his scribe, Martin Harris, begged that he might take the work to show to his family. Harris lost the translation, and Joseph had to turn to the small plates of Nephi for a record of the same time period. In coming to know the Lord, the faithful, with Nephi, must be content to sometimes say with trust, "I know that he loveth his children; nevertheless, I do not know the meaning of all things."[73]

The voice of the Lord came to Lehi by night and told him to take his journey from the valley of Lemuel deeper into the wilderness. The next day he arose and, to his great astonishment, beheld upon the ground a brass ball of curious workmanship containing two spindles. One of the spindles pointed the direction they should travel through the trackless desert, that they might keep to the more fertile parts of the wilderness. What could be more critical in a place where life hung on finding the next well, when water sources were scattered sometimes sixty miles apart in the worst parts of the waste, and where the scant vegetation shifted with every season.

In no other way could their complete dependence on the Lord during this journey be more clear, for the Liahona "did work for them according to their faith in God; therefore, if they had faith to believe that God could cause that those spindles should point the way they should go, behold, it was done; therefore they had this miracle . . . wrought by the power of God, day by day."[74] Not year by year or month by month, not occasional spirituality for this journey. They had to walk in the Lord and with Him. As with the children of Israel before them, the Lord said, "I will . . . be your light in the wilderness."[75]

As they plunged into the wilderness, they were aware that they were reenacting Israel's exodus. It was not by accident that they were leaving the world, being tested and tried in the wilderness, and would finally come to the promised land. This was God's design for His people, a type that repeated itself, each replay containing many of the elements of all the others. It is the pattern for individual spirituality, too, as the Lord asks His own to leave the world, learn their utter dependence on Him in the wilderness, and be tried and tested and finally transformed before they are eligible for the promised land. If Israel had been led by the Lord, so would Lehi's party. If Moses had talked to the Lord on the mountain, so would Nephi. If the armies of Egypt had been destroyed, so would be Jerusalem. If Israel had its complainers of fragile faith, so did Lehi in his sons Laman and Lemuel. Nephi had a keen sense of the history they were replaying and reminded them, "Let us be strong like unto Moses."[76]

Left: Morning light touches ancient, 85-foot high lock of the Marib Dam in modern Yemen, which stood from 750 B.C. until its collapse in A.D. 570. It provided water in ancient Sheba for growing crops. Lehi probably led his family southeast along the Red Sea to Nahom, probably in ancient Sheba, where they may have stopped to raise crops before turning eastward to skirt the most forbidding desert on earth.

Above: Hundreds of years of lowering water pots by rope have grooved this wood in an ancient well in Yemen. The travelers of the desert had to know of the water sources or they would perish. There are only 118 known wells along the course that parallels the Red Sea where Lehi and his family might have traveled. "The history of Arabia is written with water, not ink. Where there is water, there is life . . . and the great oases of the Arabian peninsula do not move from place to place."[77]

The desert is a lonely, brooding place where hunger, thirst, and fear are the rule. Nephi and his family would have known them all as they headed south-southeast down the miserable stretch of desert by the Red Sea. This is not a place of rest or cheer but of glum survival. Bedouins who dwell here are on a constant prowl for food, hunting on foot, scrambling to the top of craggy mountains looking for sheep, goats, oryx, or other "wild beasts."[78] Certainly, Nephi and his brothers knew this tension. Their family's survival depended on their expert hunting with bows and slings.

Nephi tells us that the Lord let them "make much fire, as [they] journeyed in the wilderness,"[79] so they "did live upon raw meat."[80] It is the desert way to kill a sheep or goat and then "eat the liver or kidney raw adding to it a little salt" or to indulge oneself in a whole slice of raw flesh. One writer notes that if the Bedouins are desperate, they " 'slaughter a camel, one of their beasts of burden, and nourish themselves like animals from the raw meat' or else scorch the flesh quickly in a small fire to soften it sufficiently not to have to gnaw it 'like dogs.' "[81] Often, exhausted after a day of travel, they throw themselves on the ground with only enough energy to eat dried dates. What pain must lie behind Nephi's understatement that "they did suffer much for the want of food."[82]

The misery was complete when after much travel, long enough for his brothers' bows to lose their spring from continual hunting, Nephi's own steel bow broke, and they "did return without food to [their] families."[83] How many days without food did they go before their anguish collapsed into full-scale murmuring and fist-shaking against the Lord? Even Lehi complained, but Nephi against great odds made a new bow and asked his father, "Whither shall I go to obtain food?"[84] The children of Israel had been fed manna in the desert; now Lehi needed his own divine help. Repentant, he prayed, and the Liahona pointed Nephi to a mountain top where he slayed wild beasts and returned with food for his family. It was a clarifying experience to remember that it was the Lord who fed them. The center point of the Exodus pattern is always the loving deliverance of the Lord.

Pages 36–37: The brightness of the afternoon sun is nearly obliterated during this sandstorm in the Arabian peninsula near the borders of the Red Sea. Driven by winds in excess of seventy miles an hour, sand particles cut with abrasive power any object or life form they touch. Bowmaking was a skill reserved to specialists in the ancient world. "The only bowwood obtainable in all Arabia was the nab wood that grew only 'amid the inaccessible and overhanging crags' of Mount Jasum and Mount Azd, which are situated in the very region . . . the broken bow incident occurred."[85] Nephi emerges as the Christ figure, the instrument of temporal and spiritual salvation.

Above: 3,000-year-old city of Baraqish on the incense trails of Sheba with two ancient tombs in the foreground. The modern name of this region is Nehem, named after the Yemini tribe who have dwelt in the area for at least a thousand years. It is hard not to observe the similarities between this place and the Nahom mentioned in Nephi's account.[86] Nahom likely comes from the Semitic root NHM, whose basic meaning is "'to comfort, console,' and . . . in Hebrew the NHM root is used extensively with reference to . . . 'mourning' the death of another."[87] Thousands of ancient graves have been discovered in this area, making this probably the largest burial site in Arabia. In such a place "the daughters of Ishmael did mourn exceedingly, because of the loss of their father."[88]

Lehi had named the river and valley where he made his first camp after Laman and Lemuel. The place of the broken bow he had called Shazar. Renaming geographical locations to suit oneself is a common Oriental custom. That is why arriving at a place already "called Nahom"[89] is noteworthy. At this point they had probably traveled far enough south in the Arabian peninsula to reach the wealthy and legendary land of Sheba. Here, perhaps, worn down by the journey or by age, Ishmael died and was buried. His daughters mourned and complained, but Laman and Lemuel began plotting in the dark abyss of their hearts to kill their father, Lehi, and brother Nephi. Their motive was power—the primordial issue, Satan's first complaint, oft repeated by his followers. Who ruled? Who was first? They said of Nephi, "He says that the Lord has talked with him, and also that angels have ministered unto him. But behold, we know that he lies unto us . . . thinking, perhaps, that he may lead us away into some strange wilderness . . . to make himself a king and a ruler over us."[90]

Afternoon clouds build, but little rain ever comes in the area of Wadi Jauf in Yemen. Pre-Islamic legends in the area speak of one Hud (or Yahud, which means Jew) who came through the region and was a prophet. He preached to them and told them of things to come. "I am sent to you by Him [the Lord] to warn you. . . . Seek forgiveness of your Lord and turn to Him in repentance. He will make a goodly provision for you . . . and will bestow His grace upon the righteous."[91] Some legends say Hud preached to a great city called Iram which rejected his words, and the city was destroyed by a great sandstorm that formed the Empty Quarter. Perhaps as Lehi traveled, if he came upon those who would hear the word, he would preach to them.

Above: View into the great Empty Quarter of the Arabian Desert. No habitation exists in this forsaken area of a quarter-of-a-million square miles. Lehi's party likely skirted the south end of this area as they made their way across the last 800 miles of the journey to Bountiful. Ancient caravans took from two to three months to cross to the Dhofar region, the area where frankincense trees were indigenous and abundant. That it took Lehi's party eight years to cross tells us much about the wilderness experience and the Lord's desire to test and try His people as He did in the days of Israel's journey from Egypt. A fuller account of their journey is included in the Large Plates of Nephi.[92]

The twenty-five hundred miles of Lehi's wilderness journey from Jerusalem to the Arabian Sea took eight years. This means the group probably stopped several times for long encampments and the growing of crops. Sariah gave birth to both Jacob and Joseph in this forsaken emptiness.

Today, Bedouins camp for ten to twelve days in a spot until the area is so soiled by the animals that the fleas and flies become unbearable. Then the Bedouins move on. However, Lehi's family probably stayed at Nahom for a much longer time, mourning Ishmael and preparing for the next leg of the journey skirting the worst, most forbidding desert of the world, the Empty Quarter, whose first recorded crossing in modern times was not until 1928. This is likely the place where Nephi said they waded through much affliction.

If they had traveled too far south of the Empty Quarter deeper into Sheba's more hospitable clime, they would have been in more

populated areas. Yet this was dangerous. Why? "The Arab tribes are in a state of almost perpetual war against each other. . . . To surprise the enemy by a sudden attack, and to plunder a camp, are chief objects of both parties."[93] "Raiding to them is the spice of life."[94] Any approaching party would be viewed with wary suspicion. Perhaps because of this danger, the Lord did not allow them to make much fire, whose light or smoke in night or day could have been spotted for many miles across the vast waste by alert enemies.[95]

Edging the Empty Quarter, then, each day would be depressingly like the last. Progress would be slow, perhaps with scouting parties sent ahead in Bedouin fashion. Traveling, the group would likely have been silent, moody, not given to the talk that would cause thirst. The differences between them might have been magnified in the boiling heat and erupted into violent anger in their camps.

Pages 42–43: Looking into the ominous, barren canyons of Wadi Sayq (pronounced sike) in modern Oman. The elevation here is over 4,000 feet and within twenty miles will drop to the ocean. In one of these feeder canyons Lehi and his party may have entered the wadi and followed the directions of the Liahona through the main canyon to the ocean. Certainly, viewing this forboding canyon, they would not have known that lush Bountiful was directly ahead. By this time the party had at least 33 individuals, likely over 100 camels, probably eight large tents (each weighing as much as 500 pounds), remaining provisions, and numerous sacks of all varieties of seeds they had brought from Jerusalem.

The wilderness journey by its very nature is grueling, pitting travelers against nature, themselves, and the limits of endurance. Yet for Nephi, Moses, or anyone on the spiritual path, the underlying truth is the same. We cannot be candidates for the promised land until we have been purged in the wilderness.

Something happens in the dust, heat, and tribulation that forever shapes us and clarifies our thinking so that we can see the true nature of things. We come to understand that our supposed sense of self-sufficiency is a sham, and that we are utterly dependent on the Lord. We have no food until He shows us where to look, no direction unless He points the way. Nephi told his brothers how the children of Israel were led: "According to his word he did lead them; and according to his word he did do all things for them; and there was not any thing done save it were by his word."[96] Not anything. Until we see this, we are blind.

It is our neediness that turns us to Christ. The atonement is only a beautiful abstraction until we feel the anguish and pain not only of sin but also of the misery attendant to mortality that Christ is willing to lift from us. As has been said, "For the happy man, prayer is only a jumble of words until the day when sorrow comes to explain to him the sublime language by means of which he speaks to God."[97] This dependence on the Lord does not mean that we are robbed of power or agency. Indeed, no one on the trip was asked to do more than Nephi—he obtained the plates, made a bow, foraged for food, scrambled to mountaintops to pray, made plates, and built a ship. Yet he intimately came to know that all he could do was not enough, for "it is by grace that we are saved, after all we can do."[98] In the wilderness, when the righteous come face to face with their limitations, they see that God is there to take up the slack.

The wilderness, then, not only proves humanity; it also proves the Lord, showing that He is as good as His word, that He can be trusted, that His loving arms are continually outstretched. "Ye shall know," said the Lord, "that it is by me that ye are led."[99]

Nephi and his brothers Laman and Lemuel lived through the same eight years in the wilderness, ate the same food, stopped at the same camps, saw the same scenery. Yet if ever a controlled environment showed the stark contrasts between fragile and stalwart faith, this was it. Nephi was the picture of constancy; neither hunger nor pain could remove his sense of the Lord's love and direction. He explained, "I know in whom I have trusted."[100]

Laman and Lemuel, however, were tossed with every wind because they knew not the Lord and therefore could not trust Him. Nothing was more important, more telling and pressing upon them than their fears, their envyings, the comforts of Jerusalem, the arm of flesh. Consequently, they could believe, but they could not hold to their belief. When Nephi brought food after making a new bow, they "did humble themselves before the Lord, and did give thanks unto him."[101] Yet, when Ishmael died, they lost faith again. Nephi pleaded with them, read to them from the plates of brass, and showed how the Lord had blessed them, but Laman and Lemuel had no memory. A miracle or blessing one day did not stay with them the next—and they were completely miserable for this deficiency.

Nephi summed up his feelings: "And so great were the blessings of the Lord upon us, . . . our women did give plenty of suck for their children, and were strong, yea, even like unto the men; and they began to bear their journeyings without murmurings. . . . And if it so be that the children of men keep the commandments of God he doth nourish them, and strengthen them, and provide means whereby they can accomplish the thing which he has commanded them."[102] For their part, Laman and Lemuel had only this whine: "We have wandered in the wilderness for these many years; and our women have toiled, being big with child; and they have borne children in the wilderness and suffered all things, save it were death; and it would have been better that they had died before they came out of Jerusalem. . . . We might have enjoyed our possessions and the land of our inheritance; yea, and we might have been happy."[103] Can they really be talking of the same experience?

Pages 44–45: Looking southwest to main lower section of Wadi Sayq in modern Oman. Even in May, the driest month of the year, when this photo was taken, the Dhofar region is lush and green with vegetation. After nearly 2,500 miles of travel in trackless waste, and now just two miles from the ocean, the hearts of Lehi and his family would have leaped for joy as greenery of Bountiful burst upon

their view. Climatically, this area is unique in all of Arabia because it is just touched by the edge of the tremendous monsoons that wreak so much destruction in Pakistan and India each year.

Above: Golden morning sun warms the sand of this isolated beach on the far southwestern coast of modern Oman. Surely this sea was "Irreantum, which,

being interpreted, is many waters."[104] The beach is nearly one mile wide and fits the description that Nephi gives of Bountiful better than any other place in Arabia. The wadi here runs year round and is full of fish that could have been easily caught for food so the brothers could turn their efforts away from hunting and focus on building a ship.

Delicate flowers shoot forth in their beauty at Wadi Sayq in Oman. Colors like these in nature had probably not been seen by Lehi's party for many years. The name Bountiful seems to be a descriptive term for a low-lying, coastal area that is abundant with fruit and fertile for growing. The name is used in the promised land for one city and two lands that evidently fit this same description.

Endure to the end,"[105] the Lord tells us, but He doesn't always tell us where the end is. How many, when patience and perseverance have been unbearably stretched, give up just five minutes too soon? Problems do not always announce that they are nearly finished. So it was for Lehi and his family. Nothing was inviting about the wadi's entrance that leads to the best possible candidate for the seashore site of Bountiful. It is a grim, steep, arid canyon where trails suddenly end in a two-hundred-foot drop. No water source is visible, and its scant vegetation clings to the wadi for its tenuous hold on life. If this was indeed the place, the party would have snaked at least fifteen miles down the canyon before their eyes saw the surprise of green. Suddenly, seemingly from nowhere, the wadi is transformed with lush jungle, gnarled trunks, and a canopy of leaves, the only area so watered in the whole Arabian peninsula. Lehi's family would have been less than a mile from the shore before they saw the ocean and sniffed the sea air. "And we beheld the sea, which we called Irreantum."[106]

Awesome evening light colors clouds and sky at remote and isolated Wadi Sayq at 16 degrees 44 minutes latitude. Is this where Nephi built the ship? Best evidence suggests it may be. There are only six potential candidates for the location, and this is the only one that fits the description given by Nephi in every particular.[107] The location of this beach is significant in that Lehi and his family would have been separated from the outside world as they prepared for their journey across the globe to the new world. Perhaps the isolation would help keep the wayward sons focused on the work at hand and kept the influence of the polytheistic cultures in the regions nearby away from their thinking. This would be their last touch with the old world as this branch of Joseph was being broken off and scattered to one of the nethermost parts of the vineyard.[108]

49

To eyes long accustomed to the burning sands, Bountiful, with its flowing springs and shady trees, must have been unspeakable relief. Behind the travelers lay the desert, before them the sea, but here, at least for now, was refuge: "We did come to the land which we called Bountiful, because of its much fruit and also wild honey; and all these things were prepared of the Lord that we might not perish. . . . We did pitch our tents by the seashore; and notwithstanding we had suffered many afflictions and much difficulty, yea, even so much that we cannot write them all, we were exceedingly rejoiced when we came to the seashore."[109]

Then one night, the voice of the Lord came to Nephi: "Arise, and get thee into the mountain."[110] Immediately Nephi went as directed to the mount, where the Lord said, "Thou shalt construct a ship, after the manner which I shall show thee, that I may carry thy people across these waters."[111] This was not to be a ship in the custom of the day, but a design of the Lord's. To the unfaithful, such a request was preposterous, a little like asking one of us to build a rocket and take off for some unknown destination in space. Nephi had no training in the intricate art of shipbuilding. This was reserved for a special group of craftsmen trained for years in the skill. Even if Nephi could build a semblance of a ship, who would guarantee its safety in the buffeting storms of the sea? Who could begin to understand where they were heading, a mystery land of unmentionable distance? Yet, what the Lord had spoken, He had spoken, and that was always enough for Nephi, who offered no protests, only a practical question: "Whither shall I go that I may find ore to molten, that I may make tools to construct the ship after the manner which thou hast shown unto me?"[112]

After the Lord had indicated where to find ore, Nephi "did make a bellows wherewith to blow the fire, of the skins of beasts,"[113] and, he wrote, "I did make tools of the ore which I did molten out of rock."[114] From the beginning, crossing the sea was a bold project undertaken by only a few other groups in the history of the ancient world. But Nephi stood on the Lord's promise: "I will prepare the way before you. . . . After ye have arrived in the promised land, ye shall know that I, the Lord, am God."[115]

Left: Western light spills over the mount and gives last touches to greenery at the seashore site of Wadi Sayq. This is a freestanding mountain next to the isolated beach and, if this is where the ship was built, then this is the most likely place Nephi would have come to receive instructions from the Lord. "And I, Nephi, did go into the mount oft, and I did pray oft unto the Lord; wherefore the Lord showed unto me great things."[116] The pattern is an invitation to all.

Above: Large trees sixty to eighty feet high grow in abundance starting about a half mile from the sea. Hardwood trees in the area include tamarindus, sycamore, and boscia. Timber would be needed for nearly every aspect of shipbuilding, including large amounts for the scaffolding and framework around the ship as well as for a large ramp for the ship to slide into the ocean. As the party was traveling along the Red Sea they could have seen local shipbuilders in their trade. Therefore, Nephi said, he "did not work the timbers after the manner of men."[117]

51

Abundant deposits of jasper (a flint-like rock) are strewn along the upper reaches of the canyon of Wadi Sayq. If two of these rocks are struck repeatedly and sharply together, they will make sparks that can be used to ignite tinder and light a fire. It may have been this kind of rock Nephi used to start a fire.[118] Throughout their lengthy journey from Jerusalem to this area, Laman and Lemuel and often the sons of Ishmael were like flint, sparking together in anger, causing fires of hot contention and murderous thoughts between them and the righteous in their family.

In the Book of Mormon, the wicked never admit their wickedness. They are perfectly, comfortably self-deceived. Pride makes them blind and therefore unrepentant. In fact, they protest their righteousness, their devotion to the commandments of God. When Nephi told Laman and Lemuel that he was about to build a ship, they showered him with derision and refused to labor, saying, "Our brother is a fool, for he thinketh that he can build a ship."[119]

If he was a fool, however, they felt they were wise: "We knew that ye could not construct a ship, for we knew that ye were lacking in judgment."[120] "And we know that the people who were in the land of Jerusalem were a righteous people; for they kept the statutes and judgments of the Lord."[121] Believe one lie, and all the other lies follow and fit. One can even contort reality to make them fit. If the Lord were not leading them and their father were a just a foolish dreamer, all their whining would seem justified. It was Laman and Lemuel's basic premise that was so faulty, and therefore is a warning to us all on our spiritual journey through the wilderness. Satan's powerful tool is the lie. Make a lie—even one you believe—the foundation of your thought, and misery follows.

Nephi reminded his brothers that they had seen an angel and heard the Lord's voice from time to time, but this did not move them. Since they didn't know God, they couldn't trust Him. They could not believe that Jerusalem would be destroyed, and therefore the entire experience of removing them from the place was to them not a blessing but a curse.

To penetrate the dark veil over their minds, Nephi began to recount what they had been taught and must know—the history of Moses and Israel. The Lord had divided the Red Sea for Israel, led them, fed them, brought water from a rock to quench their thirst. Nephi, too, had experienced the power and goodness of God. His brothers' unbelief or the day-to-day challenge of building a ship did not change this. "If God had commanded me to do all things I could do them. If he should command me that I should say unto this water, be thou earth, it should be earth. . . . And now, if the Lord has such great power, and has wrought so many miracles among the children of men, how is it that he cannot instruct me, that I should build a ship?"[122]

Looking west across one of the freshwater sources and up Wadi Sayq in Oman toward the beautiful, lush mountainsides. Nephi is careful to place in the record his feelings about the land of Bountiful: "We did come to the land which we called Bountiful, because of its much fruit and also wild honey; and all these things were prepared of the Lord that we might not perish."[123] As their food supplies were depleted to nothing, their hunger and thirst would have been foremost in their thinking at all times, and Nephi, as always, gives full credit to the Lord for preparing the way for them. Agricultural areas were discovered on the west side of the wadi area while shipbuilding took place on the east.

Above: Morning light illuminates cliffs along the shore of the Arabian Sea at the west end of the Wadi Sayq area. Significantly, the waters along the beach here are only shallow for a few short feet, and then they drop rapidly to great depths, an appropriate place to launch a ship. Nephi records that his brothers were "desirous to throw me into the depths of the sea,"[124] which seems to indicate there was a physical height, such as a cliff nearby. Cliffs line the ocean front in this area.

Right, bottom: This large and interestingly shaped stone was found not far from the possible ship site above. The stone is concave, like part of a Near Eastern oven. A shaft for air at the bottom of the stone and the center of the oven area runs about fifteen feet to the back of the large rock. Deposits of carbon cover the front of the oven area.

The guilty taketh the truth to be hard, for it cutteth them to the very center."[125] After Nephi's talk, all Laman and Lemuel wanted to do was heave him into the depths of the sea. Yet as they came forth to lay their hands on him, Nephi stopped them: "In the name of the Almighty God, I command you that ye touch me not, for I am filled with the power of God, even unto the consuming of my flesh; and whoso shall lay his hands upon me shall wither even as a dried reed."[126]

Sobered and confounded, the brothers, according to Nephi, durst not "lay their hands upon [him] nor touch [him] with their fingers"[127] for several days. Then the Lord came again to Nephi, saying, "Stretch forth thine hand again unto thy brethren, and they shall not wither before thee, but I will [shake] them."[128] Thereafter Nephi touched his brothers, and they were shaken, feeling the power of this God whom they had mocked. Only then did they say, "We know of a surety that the Lord is with thee, for we know that it is the power of the Lord that has shaken us."[129]

Now Laman and Lemuel joined Nephi in the massive project of building a ship large enough to transport perhaps thirty-five to forty people and withstand the crashing ocean waves. They had to create tools, smelt ore, cut towering trees that were further up the wadi and transport them to shore, and create some kind of a crane system and machinery to hoist the beams. Since all food supplies would have been depleted in the empty wilderness, others of their group must have been at work growing crops. This may have taken several years.

During the building project, Nephi "did go into the mount oft, and . . . did pray oft unto the Lord; wherefore the Lord showed unto [him] great things."[130] The "wherefore" is telling in this statement, explaining why the Lord showed unto him great things and how He will do the same for us. It was because Nephi pulled himself away from the distractions and demands of his life to escape to a place alone to "pray oft." In these communions, Nephi also reported that "the Lord did show [him] from time to time after what manner [he] should work the timbers of the ship."[131]

Above: View from the east end of the Wadi Sayq beach looking nearly south into the Arabian Sea. Noteworthy is the pattern of rocks shaped like a ship in the upper beach area in the foreground of this picture. It does appear that someone built a ship here. Vegetation grows readily among the rocks, further emphasizing the ship pattern. Larger buildup of rocks can also be seen at the fore, middle, and aft part of the site. The pattern measures 130 feet long and 65 feet wide at the center. Three interspersed larger piles of rocks are seen to the left middle of the picture, leading down to the high-tide position of the ocean and may have been foundation stones for a ramp to the sea.

View across the wadi area with a large man-made mound visible on the right. A double lines of stones can be seen in the picture; these run many hundreds of feet from the mound to the wadi itself and may have been the foundation of a water transportation system that could have carried timber from farther up the wadi to the ship-building site. Initial observations suggest that the ancient, fourteen-feet-high, forty-five-feet-in-diameter weathered mound could have been used for some type of waterworks to run machinery. The large outcropping of rock in the center of the picture has graffiti on it, some in a language not yet identified. Clearly some major effort took place here in ancient times. Flamingos and other wildlife delight in the abundance of Wadi Sayq.

When Nephi had completed the ship according to the Lord's design, his brothers marveled at its exceedingly fine workmanship. The time had come to leave behind everything this little community had known: their culture, their history, their geographic continuity with the children of Israel. From now on, they would be a branch "broken off"[132] from the vineyard and poignantly aware of it. Over sixty years later, long after they had settled in the promised land, Nephi's younger brother Jacob would lament, "Our lives passed away like as it were unto us a dream, we being a lonesome and a solemn people, wanderers, cast out from Jerusalem, born in tribulation, in a wilderness, and hated of our brethren . . . wherefore, we did mourn out our days."[133]

Certainly with much trepidation they gathered fruit, honey, seeds, meat from the wilderness, and boarded the ship. Then, surely with some eyes staring backward, they put forth into the sea and were driven before the wind toward the promised land.

Above: Verdant wadi flora about a quarter of a mile from the seashore. Surely this place was a respite after the grueling years in the forbidding deserts of Arabia. The Lord was very specific about how to build the ship and how to make preparations for the long journey to the promised land. "After we had prepared all things," recounted Nephi, "much fruits and meat from the wilderness, and honey in abundance, and provisions according to that which the Lord had commanded us, we did go down into the ship."[134]

Left: Ancient graffiti of yet-undetermined date on the rock face near the mound shows a ship or sailing vessel, camels, and many other items. Early observations of this archaeological site have revealed numerous double lines of stones imbedded in the earth on both sides of the wadi (one of these lines is over 600 feet long), a number of omega-shaped rock structures (perhaps for agricultural storage), a likely candidate for a well, a large retaining wall, and a grave.

Late afternoon light washes across a double line of stones that leads to the mound at Wadi Sayq. The thought of people of the desert becoming mariners seems preposterous unless we consider that they were led by the hand of the Lord. Describing the loading of the ship, Nephi notes that it was done "every one according to his age."[135] All helped in the process, each doing what he or she could with the ability and strength each had, the children carrying small amounts and the adults the heavier loads. If the sons of Ishmael increased their families during the wilderness experience, then there were at least fourteen children who entered the ship who were ten years old and younger, some teenage children in the group, and seventeen adults. By now Nephi was probably between twenty-five and thirty years old.

After they had been driven before the wind for many days through the ocean, Nephi's brothers, the sons of Ishmael, and their wives "began to make themselves merry, insomuch that they began to dance, and to sing, and to speak with much rudeness."[136] Perhaps Nephi's description implies that they were having an orgy. At any rate, the degree of sin was such that he wrote, "I began to fear exceedingly lest the Lord should be angry with us."[137] When he spoke to his brothers about it in soberness, however, they bound him with cords so tightly that he could not move, and "the compass, which had been prepared of the Lord, did cease to work. Wherefore, they knew not whither they should steer the ship."[138] Soon, a violent storm arose, "yea, a great and terrible tempest, and we were driven back upon the waters for the space of three days; and they began to be frightened exceedingly lest they should be drowned in the sea; nevertheless they did not loose me."[139]

While the storm raged, Lehi and Sariah, "were near to be cast

with sorrow into a watery grave."[140] Nothing would soften Laman and Lemuel's hearts, not Nephi's wife with her prayers and tears, not his children's pleas. Nephi admits frankly, "There was nothing save it were the power of God, which threatened them with destruction, could soften their hearts."[141] Finally, after the fourth day driven back, when they were about to be swallowed in the depths of the sea, Nephi's brothers "began to see that the judgments of God were upon them"[142] and that they would surely perish unless they loosed Nephi. Nephi's wrists and ankles were swollen and sore. "Nevertheless," he says, "I did look unto my God, and I did praise him all the day long."[143]

With Nephi loose, "there was a great calm,"[144] the compass worked again, and he "did guide the ship, that we sailed again towards the promised land."[145] Like the dividing of the Red Sea, like the waters of baptism, being saved in the water is an integral part of the wilderness pattern.

Pulling away from Wadi Sayq, we see the raised ship-like pattern of rocks on the shore at the center of the picture with the piles of rocks leading to the water also visible. The huge rock at the top of the lighter-colored beach has the ancient graffiti, and the possible foundry stone can be seen just to the lower left of the large rock. In the perfect patterns of the Lord, the foreordained day of their departure arrived: "It came to pass that the voice of the Lord came unto my father, that we should arise and go down into the ship."[146] The four-times-repeated phrase "go down into the ship" reminds us of that critical part of the exodus pattern, the water experience, the baptism, the coming through the waters in the wilderness. When the true history books are opened, the expedition of Lehi's family, more than twenty centuries before Columbus, will be counted as one of the greatest journeys of all time.

2 THIS PRECIOUS LAND OF PROMISE

From Jerusalem, Lehi's party had made an epic journey covering two-thirds of the globe across the Pacific Ocean, probably to the western shores of Central America. This was the promised land, reserved only for those of many nations whom the Lord would bring here. In contrast to the desert lands they had known, here was so much abundance that in a bold move they planted all the seeds they had so carefully brought with them from Jerusalem and "they did grow exceedingly."[1] In the forests were "beasts . . . of every kind."[2]

The land came with a covenant blessing and cursing, remembered and often mentioned by Lehi's posterity: "This land is consecrated unto him whom he shall bring. And if . . . they shall serve him according to the commandments . . . it shall be a land of liberty unto them; wherefore, they shall never be brought down into captivity. . . . But behold . . . if the day shall come that they will reject the Holy One of Israel, the true Messiah . . . , behold, the judgments of him that is just shall rest upon them."[3]

Pages 60–61: Majestic light touches clouds and water framing the promised land that the people of Nephi would come to know. Here, near modern Fronteras on Lago de Izabal in Guatemala, may have been the southeastern boundaries of the Nephite lands. Upon arrival, the family of Lehi would have had to clear jungle land to build their civilization.

Left: Beautiful lagoons dot the jungles of Central America and to this day offer places for habitation with easy access to fishing and hunting to sustain life. The Book of Mormon is not a history of the American Indian but a lineage account of a particular family and people. The largely religious history certainly cannot be considered a comprehensive account of everything that was taking place in the area.

Above: Even during the dry season (November to April) in Mesoamerica, beautiful flora grow with vibrant colors. Many places receive between 60 and 100 inches of rain a year and do not have great diversities in temperature.

Above: Seedling of a pine taking root on the red soil of an evergreen cloud forest of Guatemala. This land has at least eleven different ecosystems, each with its own characteristics, sometimes separated only by a mountain ridge, moving from very dry to very fertile within only one or two miles. Tropical rain forests cover much of the area, though the ecosystems range from mangrove swamps to pine-oak liquidambar and tropical deciduous forests.

Right: Two mighty Ceiba trees anchored firmly at ancient site of Quirigua near the border of Guatemala and Honduras. The ancient Maya, who are possible candidates for the remnants of the Lamanites, believed the Ceiba to be a sacred tree, the Tree of Life, standing in the very center of the earth. The great tree, in their traditions, connected the thirteen heavens with the nine levels of the underworld, its branches reaching high to brush with the heavens and its roots reaching deep into the dark underworld.

Lehi and his family had come to the promised land, but contrary to popular thought, it may not have been an unpopulated, pristine land. Abundant archaeological and linguistic evidence suggest that other people were already present in the area, though their populations were probably scattered and weak.[4] We certainly get this sense later in the record when Jacob describes an outsider, saying, "There came a man among the people of Nephi, whose name was Sherem. . . . And . . . he had a perfect knowledge of the language of the people."[5] Among those in the area may have been the Olmecs, widely considered to be the mother culture of Mesoamerica and perhaps related to the Jaredites. Though the main Jaredite population lived north of the narrow neck of land and their power would collapse in civil war sometime between 600 and 300 B.C., survivors continued beyond that time and played a predominant role in shaping the civilization of Lehi's posterity in this new land. Most scholars believe that to understand the population of ancient Mesoamerica with its more than two hundred languages,[6] one has to assume there must have been multiple migrations from many groups of people. In such circumstances, Lehi and his family, would be just one lineage group.

Lehi was nearing death when he received a vision that Jerusalem had indeed been destroyed. Babylonia had swept in somewhere between 590 and 586 B.C. and killed or carried off the leaders of the population. King Zedekiah's eyes had been put out in the desert. It had been a scene of carnage and certain death or slavery the Lehites had been spared by the Lord.

Near his death, Lehi, describing himself as a "trembling parent,"[7] had blessings for his posterity. To Jacob, born in the tribulation of the wilderness, he gave the message that in the Lord's plan, "there is an opposition in all things."[8]

Adam and Eve in the garden were in a state of innocence, "having no joy, for they knew no misery; doing no good, for they knew no sin."[9] This opposition was so that having agency, people could experience both bitter and sweet and then choose for themselves. "Wherefore, men are free . . . to choose liberty and eternal life, through the great Mediator of all men, or to choose captivity and death."[10]

Beautiful Mayan inscriptions carved on stairs at the great city of Palenque, in the state of Chiapas in southern Mexico. Though Palenque is generally considered younger than Book of Mormon times, dating from A.D. 600–800, it is a reminder that Mesoamerica was the only place on the continent that had a written language before the coming of the Europeans and thus is the most likely candidate for the homeland of Lehi's posterity. The principles used in glyphic writings of Mesoamerica are essentially the same as that of the Egyptians. One of the glyphs discovered in seventh century Palenque has recently been interpreted as "and then it came to pass." This same or similar phrase occurs 1,381 times in the Book of Mormon.

In the blessing to his son, little Joseph, Lehi looked to the distant future and what would become of their posterity. As a reference he used the record of Joseph of Egypt contained on the brass plates but mostly lost to us today.[11] Lehi said, "Great were the covenants of the Lord which he made unto Joseph. Wherefore, Joseph truly saw our day. And he obtained a promise of the Lord, that out of the fruit of his loins the Lord God would raise up a righteous branch unto the house of Israel . . . to be broken off."[12]

With the remarkable precision of revelation, in this record Joseph also referred to Joseph Smith and his mission twenty-four centuries later. "A seer," Joseph wrote, "shall the Lord my God raise up."[13] "And his name shall be called after me; and it shall be after the name of his father."[14] This seer would join the record of Joseph's posterity that Lehi and his family would keep (the Book of Mormon), with the record of Judah (the Bible) in the last days "unto the confounding of false doctrines."[15]

The Book of Mormon would come forth in a day when plain and precious things had been removed from the Bible. "At the time the book proceeded out of the mouth of the Jew, the things which were written were plain and pure, and most precious and easy to the understanding of all men."[16] But "behold, they have taken away from the gospel of the Lamb many parts which are plain and most precious; and also many covenants of the Lord have they taken away . . . and . . . because of these things which are taken away out of the gospel of the Lamb, an exceedingly great many do stumble, yea, insomuch that Satan hath great power over them."[17]

What a wealth of plain and precious things are lost from the Bible, including the fact that Jesus Christ and His gospel were known by the righteous in every dispensation, the plan of salvation, the meaning of the atonement, "the nature of the Godhead, . . . the purpose of mortality, . . . the workings of the Holy Spirit, the ordinances and performances that pertain to salvation, the destiny of the earth, . . . the eternity of the marriage relationship, . . . the eternal nature of the family,"[18] and work for the dead. The records that Lehi's family would keep and revelation brought forth by Joseph Smith in the last days would restore these truths to the earth.

Above: Tree-covered mountains in the state of Huehuetenango near the border of Mexico and Guatemala. The Book of Mormon refers a number of times to parties who became lost in the wilderness.[19] Dense jungle growth soon covers the tracks of travelers here, and in the mountainous terrain tracks are quickly washed away in an afternoon downpour.

Pages 68–69: The Sierra Los Cuchumatanes mountain range in Guatemala is a formidable boundary running from the Bay of Honduras (the Caribbean Sea) on the east to the Sierra Madre range and the Pacific Ocean on the west. The rugged, steep Cuchumatanes soar over 10,000 feet above sea level. It is easy to visualize the similarities between this and the narrow strip of wilderness that separated the Nephites on the north from the Lamanites on the south.[20] Only a few passes cross this range, all of which could have been strategic military defense positions for the Nephites.

So many times in the past, Laman and Lemuel had been on the verge of murdering Nephi. Now, with Lehi's death, surely Nephi's life was in constant danger. In the small plates he poured out his soul, wrung out by his own sins, the peril of his situation before his "enemies," and the situation that was coming to a head with his brothers.

He wrote, "My soul delighteth in the things of the Lord; and my heart pondereth continually upon the things which I have seen and heard." Yet, because he had tasted the sweetness of God's love, he was all the more aware of his weaknesses. "Nevertheless, notwithstanding the great goodness of the Lord, in showing me his great and marvelous works, my heart exclaimeth: O wretched man that I am! . . . I am encompassed about, because of the temptations and the sins which do so easily beset me. And when I desire to rejoice, my heart groaneth because of my sins."

Still, even amid these groanings, he did not allow himself to sink but instead grasped onto all he had experienced with the Lord, reaching for memory, a pattern for the rest of us when despair would take us: "Nevertheless, I know in whom I have trusted. My God hath been my support; he hath led me through mine afflictions in the wilderness; and he hath preserved me upon the waters of the great deep. He hath filled me with his love, even unto the consuming of my flesh. He hath confounded mine enemies, unto the causing of them to quake before me. Behold, he hath heard my cry by day, and he hath given me knowledge by visions in the night-time. . . .

"O then, if I have seen so great things, if the Lord in his condescension unto the children of men hath visited men in so much mercy, why should my heart weep and my soul linger in the valley of sorrow. . . . And why should I yield to sin, because of my flesh? . . . Awake my soul! No longer droop in sin. Rejoice, O my heart, and give place no more for the enemy of my soul. . . . O Lord, wilt thou encircle me around in the robe of thy righteousness! O Lord, wilt thou make a way for mine escape before mine enemies? . . . O Lord, I have trusted in thee, and I will trust in thee forever."[21]

*Above: The Nephites may have been famil-
iar with this common sight of the beautiful red bromeliad, an epiphyte. Epiphytes
are so-called air plants and use their roots
only to tightly anchor themselves. Having
no contact with soil, they get all their
nourishment from wind-blown dust and
the minerals carried in rainwater. Jacob
taught, "Cleave unto God as he cleaveth
unto you."[22]*

*Right: Afternoon light touches hillsides
and the archeological site of Mixco
(pronounced meesh-ko) Viejo, a formidable ancient city located on the south side
of the Motagua River. We may surmise
that Nephi used the Liahona to guide the
faithful to a place like this where they
could build a city and use natural protection to defend themselves from their enemies. "Contrary to what one might expect
small groups that carry cultures to remote
and lonely places do not revert to primitive and simple ways, but become fiercely
and increasingly loyal to their original
culture."[23] Structures restored and now
visible date from the 11th century A.D.*

The depth of Nephi's peril was made clear when the Lord came
to him and warned him to flee into the wilderness. He took
his own family and Zoram, Sam, Jacob, Joseph, his sisters, and all
who believed in "the warnings and the revelations of God."[24] From
this division would grow two great nations, the Nephites and
Lamanites, who would be at each other's throats for centuries to
come. From generation to generation, the Lamanites would carry
this chip on their shoulders, that they had been wronged in the
wilderness and on the sea, their right to rule and their precious
records stolen away. It would be over 500 years before many of
them would accept the gospel again.

Nephi led his group away from the coast inland to the mountains. They called their new land Nephi, built a temple on the order
of Solomon's, sowed seeds, and "began to raise flocks, and . . .
lived after the manner of happiness."[25] The Lamanites became "an
idle people, full of mischief and subtlety, and did seek in the wilderness for beasts of prey."[26]

Jacob's tremendous talent as a teacher must have been evident early on to Nephi, so Jacob was consecrated to teach the people "the word of God with all diligence."[27] "And we did magnify our office unto the Lord,"[28] Jacob recorded. So, near the age of thirty, Jacob distilled his testimony about the atonement of Jesus Christ in a masterful discourse. He preached to the people on two consecutive days, the night between them receiving instruction from an angel who told Jacob that the name of the Son of God should be Christ[29] and shared remarkable details of the Lord's mortal life—five hundred and fifty years before He would be born. Jesus would do many miracles, but because of "priestcrafts and iniquities, they at Jerusalem [would] stiffen their necks against him, that he be crucified."[30] Though the world regards the gospel of Jesus Christ as bursting upon the scene as a radical new doctrine during His mortal life, Jacob told us, "We had a hope of his glory many hundred years before his coming; and not only we ourselves . . . but also all the holy prophets which were before us."[31]

Jacob then explained the atonement and resurrection, exclaiming, "O how great the plan of our God!"[32] The word *plan* is reassuring to us in the last days; behind what appears to be the chaos of the world is a masterful, perfect, holy plan. When we entered into the world both physical and spiritual death came upon us. This is bondage, an "awful monster,"[33] and without a plan for escape we would become "angels to a devil . . . shut out from the presence of God,"[34] mired in inescapable sins because of the demands of justice. Yet Christ provided deliverance, sparing us from the effects of physical death through the resurrection and from spiritual death through the atonement. We are freed from the grasp of justice through the mercy of Jesus Christ. Deliverance from bondage through Christ is the single greatest theme that runs through the Book of Mormon, repeated both in sermon and in actual events. The people are told about it, and then they see it in their own lives and history as individuals and communities are placed in bondage and then delivered through the Lord's grace. In many cases, the literal burden on their back is lifted. The recorders clearly do not want us to miss the message.

Left: View of Motagua River basin looking west, possibly an east-west transportation corridor of the Book of Mormon peoples. "Come," the Lord would invite us through Jacob, "every one that thirsteth, come ye to the waters."[35] One of the waters we are invited to partake of is baptism. "Come forth out of the waters of Judah, or out of the waters of baptism."[36]

Above: Beautiful hibiscus common to Central America. Hummingbirds of many varieties gather the nectar from flowers like these. In the Stela 5 "Tree of Life" stone at Izapa (see page 30), two hummingbirds have attached their beaks to the two-headed serpent, a likely representative motif of Christ. In nature some hummingbirds will do this very thing, attaching their beaks to a tree during the winter and then becoming dormant, as if they are dead, in a state of hibernation. When spring arrives, they are rejuvenated and fly on their way. This can be seen as a symbol of the power of the resurrection.

Beautiful evergreen trees grow in rich abundance in many areas of Mesoamerica. Other trees of the region include cedars, sapodillas, rosewood, breadnuts, and mahoganies—all of which could have been used in the building of the temple in the city of Nephi. "I did teach my people to build buildings, and to work in all manner of wood. . . . And I, Nephi, did build a temple; and I did construct it after the manner of the temple of Solomon . . . and the workmanship thereof was exceedingly fine."[37]

T hroughout the Book of Mormon, prophets affirmed to the people so far from their father's homeland that they were not cut off from the Lord, nor from the powerful covenants the Lord made with the house of Israel. The great prophet Isaiah, who lived less than a hundred years before Lehi, became a sort of bridge for Lehi's posterity to that spiritual heritage. Nephi exhorted his people, "ye who are a remnant of the house of Israel, a branch who have been broken off; hear ye the words of the prophet, which were written unto all the house of Israel, and liken them unto yourselves, that ye may have hope as well as your brethren from whom ye have been broken off; for after this manner has the prophet written."[38]

Nephi recorded many chapters of Isaiah's words in the small plates to "more fully persuade [his people] to believe in the Lord their Redeemer"[39] and to teach them the great patterns of the Lord in the scattering and gathering of His people, Israel. "For, behold, I have refined thee, I have chosen thee in the furnace of affliction."[40] "And I will preserve thee,"[41] the Lord said through Isaiah. Think of the reassurance these words would be to this people who never lost the sense that they were cast out from Jerusalem. "Can a woman forget her sucking child, that she should not have compassion on the son of her womb? Yea, they may forget, yet will I not forget thee, O house of Israel. Behold, I have graven thee upon the palms of my hands."[42]

Nephi taught his people through the words of Isaiah that the exile and scattering of Israel, of which they were a part, was a foreordained pattern of the Lord in saving the world. Exiled Israel would intermingle with the world and thereby give all nations a claim to the covenants of the Lord. The Lord had promised Abraham that "in thy seed after thee (that is to say, the literal seed, or the seed of the body) shall all the families of the earth be blessed, even with the blessings of the Gospel, which are the blessings of salvation, even of life eternal."[43] Through Isaiah the Lord assured all of Israel that great blessings would accompany their homecoming, or returning to God, and all would say exultantly, "Behold, God is my salvation; I will trust, and not be afraid; for the Lord Jehovah is my strength and my song."[44]

Above: Conifer forests cover many of the mountains in the state of Quezaltenango in Guatemala. These forests are south of the narrow range of mountains, the Cuchumatanes, and could have been areas of hunting and habitation for the Lamanites. Within a short time after the division of Lehi's family, the lifestyles of the Nephites and the Lamanites also became radically different. The Nephites were industrious and labored with their hands. The Lamanites, on the other hand, became an idle people. Significantly, the Lamanites are nearly always more than twice as numerous as the Nephites through the thousand-year history.

Left: New life bursts forth with an array of colors near Tonala in southern Mexico close to the Pacific Ocean. The Nephites learned how to use plants to treat sicknesses among them. "And there were some who died with fevers, which at some seasons of the year were very frequent in the land because of the climate." But, they wrote, God had prepared plants and roots to heal them.[45]

Late afternoon light touches the Peten Jungle, highlighting the great Mayan temples I, II, and IV at Tikal. Temple IV (right) stands 212 feet high and is the tallest aboriginal structure in Mesoamerica (yet discovered and restored). Tikal, located near Flores, Guatemala, was a major city of the Maya and was founded sometime around 600 B.C. It covered an area of perhaps 50 square miles and supported an ancient population of 50,000 or more. More than 3,000 buildings have been identified at Tikal in this thick, tropical rain forest. If sites are not kept clear of vegetation, they are soon swallowed up again in the undergrowth. They can vanish in only a few years. This helps explain why Mesoamerican cultures are so mysterious and little known.

W hy are the most devout and disciplined believers in every age a despised and persecuted minority, regarded by society as a whole as religious renegades?[46] It is because the world's ways are not God's ways. They are a "standing rebuke"[47] to each other, and the arguments used against the righteous in every age are remarkably the same and therefore important to know. This is why among the few things Nephi recorded for us from his personal ministry were the sophisticated, intellectual, and utterly false rebukes the worldly hurled at the believers. They are the so-called "wise" who so value themselves as being intellectually superior that they cannot be taught. The Lord says that "no man knoweth of his ways save it be revealed unto him,"[48] yet the worldly are too vain to be taught, unwilling to admit a source beyond themselves. Because of vanity, they cannot "believe that man doth not comprehend all the things which the Lord can comprehend."[49] This is why that great intellectual Sherem who came among the people during

Jacob's ministry could say with bravado that "no man knoweth" of the coming of Christ "for he cannot tell of things to come."[50] It is, he would say, against reason. Where is the empirical evidence?

"O the vainness, and the frailties, and the foolishness of men! When they are learned they think they are wise, and they hearken not unto the counsel of God, for they set it aside, supposing they know of themselves."[51] To them, man is the measure of all things.

Voices with these messages will fill the last days: First, "there is no God today, for the Lord and the Redeemer hath done his work."[52] Second, "this day he is not a God of miracles."[53] Third, "eat, drink, and be merry, for tomorrow we die."[54] Fourth, "eat, drink, and be merry; nevertheless, fear God—he will justify in committing a little sin."[55] Though the world gives the pretext of seeking knowledge, when Nephi's record comes to them, many say, "We have received the word of God, and we need no more of the word of God, for we have enough!"[56]

In his mountaintop home so far from Jerusalem, Nephi was told by the Lord that He would not forget this people who were a part of the covenant of Israel. Yet the Lord also taught, "Know ye not that there are more nations than one? . . . Wherefore, I speak the same words unto one nation like unto another . . . and they shall write it."[57] This is not a God who cares for only one tribe of people, one lineage. Ultimately He "covenanteth with none save it be with them that repent and believe in his Son, who is the Holy One of Israel."[58]

In a world where none are good but God, repentance is the important work of everyone. There are not some righteous and some wicked, forever separated and poles apart, for all have fallen short and would be left forever cut off from God were it not for the tender mercies of Jesus Christ. Continual repentance is both the gift and the pressing necessity of mortality. No wonder this, then, is central to Nephi's message: "We talk of Christ, we rejoice in Christ, we preach of Christ, we prophesy of Christ."[59]

The way of happiness is to "follow the Son, with full purpose of heart,"[60] which means casting off the impulses of the world. Who in the world celebrates humility, long-suffering, loving one's enemy, patience, faith, submitting one's will to the Lord? Who willingly gives up self-importance, class distinction, envy, and fear? Yet this is what the Lord teaches, and "the words of Christ will tell [us] all things [that we] should do."[61] If Jesus Christ was baptized, so must we be. If He submitted His will to the Father, so must we. After repentance, baptism is the gate, and "strait and narrow" is the "path which leads to eternal life."[62]

Nephi wrote, "After ye have gotten into this strait and narrow path, I would ask if all is done? . . . Nay . . . ye must press forward with a steadfastness in Christ, having a perfect brightness of hope, and a love of God and of all men. Wherefore, if ye shall press forward, feasting upon the word of Christ, and endure to the end, behold, thus saith the Father: Ye shall have eternal life."[63]

As Nephi neared the end of his record on the small plates, his writing became more anxious. He had taught his people, yet many had hardened their hearts. He wrote, "I pray continually for them by day, and mine eyes water my pillow by night."[64]

Left: Looking north as restored walls at Mixco Viejo catch late afternoon light. Nephi probably lived to be between seventy and seventy-five years old. His closing witness was poignant: "Farewell until that great day shall come . . . and you and I shall stand face to face before his bar; and ye shall know that I have been commanded of him to write these things, notwithstanding my weakness."[65]

Above: Lone plant at Mixco Viejo catches the last glow of the sun with buds ready to open within two days. Jacob, Nephi's younger brother who was born somewhere in the Arabian peninsula, took over the spiritual leadership of his people, "having first obtained [his] errand from the Lord."[66] Jacob, like his brother, had seen the Lord,[67] and he wrote, "We search the prophets, and we have many revelations and the spirit of prophecy," "and having all these witnesses we obtain a hope, and our faith becometh unshaken, insomuch that we truly can command in the name of Jesus and the very trees obey us, or the mountains, or the waves of the sea."[68]

Fifty-five years had passed since Lehi left Jerusalem, and the people had loved Nephi "exceedingly, he having been a great protector for them, having wielded the sword of Laban in their defence, and having labored in all his days for their welfare."[69] In fact, to remember him, the people called those who reigned after him "second Nephi, third Nephi, and so forth."[70] To Jacob, his faithful younger brother and now spiritual leader of the people, Nephi left the small plates with a charge that he should engrave the sacred revelations and prophecies of his people.

Yet Jacob started as Nephi ended, anxious and sick at heart about the people. They had separated themselves from the Lamanites to live a purer, higher life, but now they had slid. "It . . . causeth me to shrink with shame . . . that I must testify unto you concerning the wickedness of your hearts,"[71] he said. In the wilderness, deprivation had helped humble their fathers. But in this new land, many of them had begun to search for gold, silver, and precious ores. Jacob reprimanded them: "Because some of you have obtained more abundantly than that of your brethren ye are lifted up in the pride of your hearts, and wear stiff necks and high heads because of the costliness of your apparel, and persecute your brethren because ye suppose that ye are better than they."[72]

The evil that caused Jacob such anguish was pride, the scrambling to get above another. It was not just that people wanted things; they also wanted more of them than their fellows, dividing from one another with enmity instead of uniting in love and service. Pride is seeing the world as a race where only the fit survive by grabbing for the goods and belittling those too weak for the game. Others are seen as competitors to be stepped on, cheated, and overcome instead of as brothers and sisters to be loved.

To the Lord, "one being is as precious in his sight as the other."[73] Equality and oneness of heart mark His kingdom. "Think of your brethren like unto yourselves," Jacob pleaded, "and be familiar with all and free with your substance, that they may be rich like unto you."[74] "Before ye seek for riches, seek ye for the kingdom of God."[75]

Enos recorded his experience hunting beasts in the forest: "My soul hungered; and I kneeled down before my Maker, and I cried unto him in mighty prayer and supplication for mine own soul."[76] As Nephi had commanded that nothing be inscribed upon the small plates except those things "considered to be most precious,"[77] the story of Enos is a priceless example of the process of coming "unto the Lord with all your heart," and working "out your own salvation with fear and trembling before him."[78] Jacob's example had powerful effects upon his son: "The words which I had often heard my father speak concerning eternal life, and the joy of the saints, sunk deep into my heart."[79] Enos prayed all day, wrestling in the spirit. "And when the night came," he wrote, "I did still raise my voice high that it reached the heavens. And there came a voice unto me, saying: Enos, thy sins are forgiven thee. . . . And I . . . knew that God could not lie; wherefore, my guilt was swept away."[80] If we know that God cannot lie, then we, as Enos, can exercise great faith in Him.

Pages 80–81: Looking nearly west across restored Mayan walls of Mixco Viejo. Fifty-four verses in the Book of Mormon give some detail about the land or the city of Nephi. The Nephites likely lived in the land of Nephi for over 350 years before Mosiah was warned to flee. Here Zeniff, Noah, and Limhi ruled during Lamanite-occupied times from 200 B.C. to nearly 120 B.C. Here Alma was converted. Here Lamoni's father lived. The last mention of the land or city of Nephi is in about 63 B.C. when the Lamanites were once again occupying that land.

Left: Light filters through thick forest at Champay in Guatemala. Enos may not have known his grandfather Lehi but surely would have known and loved his uncle Nephi. Enos's father, Jacob, taught him in "his own language, and also in the nurture and admontion of the Lord."[81] The Book of Mormon royal family are educated in both secular and religious learning.[82]

Above: Deer abound in the forests of Guatemala. Some Indians may have owned, herded, and ridden them like horses.[83]

From 544 to 130 B.C., eight different record keepers kept the small plates of Nephi, passed down usually from father to son as a sacred responsibility. From Jacob and then Enos, they went to Jarom, Omni, Amaron, Chemish, Abinadom, and Amaleki, none of whom wrote much. In fact, Chemish said he saw his brother, Amaron, write his few words "in the day that he delivered them to me."[84] During this same period, the large plates containing the social and political history of the people were kept by the kings and are not contained in the Book of Mormon.

What we are left with, then, is some four hundred years of near silence with only the sketchiest clues about the history of the people of Nephi. We know they "multiplied exceedingly, and spread upon the face of the land."[85] They became rich in gold, silver, and precious things, expert in workmanship of wood, iron, copper, brass, and steel. They made weapons of war and all manner of tools to till the earth. "They observed to keep the law of Moses . . . and the laws of the land were exceedingly strict."[86]

Meanwhile, the Lamanites were a constant scourge, "and they were exceedingly more numerous" than the Nephites, perhaps because they had intermingled with populations already present in the area. With their superior cultural background and need to rule, they could easily have dominated indigenous groups. "And they loved murder and would drink the blood of beasts."[87]

In the never-ending wars with the Lamanites, the Lord protected the righteous as He promised He would. The pattern was as it had been before: when things got bad at home, the righteous were simply removed. Sometime before 200 B.C., Mosiah I was warned by the Lord that he should flee out of the land of Nephi and take as many as would "hearken unto the voice of the Lord."[88] These people who had carried the wilderness in their blood escaped there again, this time down into the land of Zarahemla. Here they met the people of Mulek, whose fathers had also come out of Jerusalem at the time of Zedekiah. Without sacred records, their language had become corrupted, and they denied the existence of their creator. The two groups joined together, and Mosiah became their king.

Mosiah's son, King Benjamin, had routed the Lamanites out of the land of Zarahemla early in his reign, and for years the people had lived in peace. Now, in about 124 B.C., as his life was about to end, he had a final blessing to bestow upon them and called them together in a great assembly. Pilgrims gathered with their families from great distances, pitching their tents with the door toward the temple. King Benjamin had a tower especially built that all might hear.

In ancient new-year celebrations like this one in the old world, the king was proclaimed as a god of the earth.[89] One would expect, too, that a people who had conquered their traditional enemies would be lauded with congratulations. They were the victors, the mighty, the powerful, vanquishing nation. What an opportunity for bravado! Yet, noticeably, starkly, quite the opposite happened here.

Far from being a king with godlike powers, Benjamin asserted that he was subject to all manner of infirmities, and, he said, "I, myself, have labored with mine own hands that I might serve you . . . [for] when ye are in the service of your fellow beings ye are only in the service of your God."[90] Then he went on frankly to tell his people that they were to be "awakened . . . to a sense of [their] nothingness, and [their] worthless and fallen state."[91] Is this any way to build a nation? Was he trying to destroy their self-esteem, their pride?

He continued, "If you should render all the thanks and praise which your whole soul has power to possess, to that God who has created you . . . and is preserving you from day to day, by lending you breath, that ye may live and move and do according to your own will, and even supporting you from one moment to another . . . yet ye would be unprofitable servants."[92]

These were the people of the Lord, so if Benjamin sounded quite different from a worldly king at a national gathering, we are meant to learn something deep. The world teaches the ways of the natural man: proudly self-contained, self-made, self-congratulatory, believing that his success depends on himself, though he is often miserably, quietly insecure for it. Benjamin told his people outright, "The natural man is an enemy to God, and has been from the fall of Adam."[93]

Pages 84–85: Clouds capture evening light in Chiapas, Mexico. It is poignant that Nephi made the small plates thirty years after leaving Jerusalem. As he wrote, he had already lost his parents, was separated from his older brothers, was living in a new land, and was nearly fifty. Surely his feelings were deep as he abridged the experiences of the past thirty years.

Above: Jungle flora such as this in the cloud forest twenty miles south of Coban, Guatemala, could have been common in the lands of the Book of Mormon. Significantly, according to archaeological evidence to date, the Maya seem to have originated in the highlands of Guatemala sometime around 600 B.C.

Right: Morning fog enwraps the karst topography of the lowland jungles near Playa Grande in Guatemala. Seventy-six verses in the Book of Mormon paint a picture of the city and land of Zarahemla, to which all roads led "down." Thus, it was probably located in a lowland area. It was also strategic politically as the capital city and religious center of the Nephites.

Giant 150–foot breadnut tree of the canopy jungle in lowlands of northern Guatemala near the border of Mexico. It is noteworthy that at the gathering to hear Benjamin's farewell address, every family had its own tent—a remnant feature of the Bedouin-desert world their ancestors came from nearly 480 years before. The transcendent message of Benjamin's address is that "whosoever should believe that Christ should come, the same might receive remission of their sins, and rejoice with exceedingly great joy, even as though he had already come among them."[94]

Even self-pity, self-consciousness, and lack of self-esteem are forms of self-importance, putting self instead of Christ at our soul's center. Only when we break that mirror of self-importance can we clearly see something beyond ourselves. The very dust we are made of belongs to Him and is sustained by Him. Yet those who are full of themselves have no room left to become full of the Lord. It is a full-time job, absorbing all our energies, to protect ourselves, watch out for ourselves, and control the world so we don't hurt ourselves, and finally no one succeeds at it. Only when we let go of that preoccupation can we turn our eyes someplace higher, let go of our pretensions, and open up to God. Benjamin taught us of our "nothingness" so we might "come to a knowledge of the goodness of God, and his matchless power, and his wisdom, and his patience, and his long-suffering towards the children of men."[95]

This is the God who stands with His arms outstretched, offering His awesome love to us through the Atonement. Yet we are blind to this love until we truly see our fallen state and run fully into our own limitations. Only then, in utmost, heartfelt need, do we bow before Him, able to feel and understand the immensity of His love and sacrifice, eager to give all that we have and are in return.

Even still, we fall short: "He doth require that ye should do as he hath commanded you; for which if ye do, he doth immediately bless you; and therefore he hath paid you. And ye are still indebted unto him, and are, and will be, forever and ever."[96]

Hearing this, King Benjamin's assembly fell to the earth, crying, "O have mercy, and apply the atoning blood of Christ."[97] Then the Spirit of the Lord came upon them, and they were filled with unspeakable joy. How ironic that they should find joy by learning of their nothingness compared to God, while those in this secular century so steeped in their own importance feel so much misery. Benjamin's people said, "The Spirit of the Lord Omnipotent . . . has wrought a mighty change in us, or in our hearts, that we have no more disposition to do evil, but to do good continually."[98] That day they entered into a covenant with God and became the "children of Christ," spiritually begotten of Him and "changed through faith on his name."[99]

Stela of Mayan warrior-leader Pacal located at Palenque in the state of Chiapas in Southern Mexico. For many years it was thought that the Maya were a peaceful people, but archaeological evidence now points nearly the opposite direction. When Mosiah, the father of Benjamin, fled out of the land of Nephi and brought those who would "hearken unto the voice of the Lord"[100] to Zarahemla, there was surely some concern over who should rule this now mixed population of the people of Zarahemla and the Nephites. The Nephites were not nearly as numerous as the people of Zarahemla, yet Mosiah was selected as ruler. Perhaps it was restiveness among those of other bloodlines who could have been rulers that stirs contention in the Book of Mormon. It is clear in the record that all are keenly aware of their own bloodlines.[101]

Above: In a three-room temple at Bonampak in Mexico, murals give a realistic view of ancient royalty, ritual preparations, the taking of captives, and victory. The finely dressed men here seem reminiscent of the wicked priests in King Noah's court in the city of Nephi. The record's description of the wicked king is clear: he did not honor his parents; he was lustful, an adulterer, promiscuous; he regularly committed whoredoms; he was greedy, prideful, lazy, idolatrous, somewhat paranoid, riotous, and drunken. With all of that, his response to the prophet Abinadi was: "Who is Abinadi, that I and my people should be judged of him?"[102]

Right: Fortress-like setting at Mixco Viejo in Guatemala as afternoon light rims the cliff edges. The people of the city of Nephi under King Noah felt strong and safe from their enemies. "They did boast in their own strength, saying that their fifty could stand against thousands of the Lamanites."[103] The wicked are always characterized by self-deception.

After King Benjamin's address, a flashback in the Book of Mormon narrative recounts a major event that happened during Mosiah I's reign at about 200 B.C. A man named Zeniff was overzealous to repossess the land of Nephi and led a group many days, "wandering" up through the wilderness toward the land of their inheritance. For many, this could have had all the emotional pull of going home; perhaps even their own lands and dwellings were still there, abandoned when they had left quickly with Mosiah. Then, too, Zarahemla may have been in the hot, muggy lowlands where the climate posed a challenge they did not face in the cooler land of Nephi.

Despite the attraction of the land of Nephi, the journey was arduous. Between Zarahemla and the land of Nephi was a "narrow strip of wilderness," perhaps a mountain range, that would always be a formidable barrier between them where passes were few and terrain was complex and exhausting. Once in Nephi, however, the Lamanite king allowed them to move into a portion of the land without protest, and they started at once to build buildings and repair the walls of the city. Why repair walls? This may tell us that the Lord had warned Mosiah to leave because the city was going to be sacked. With Lehi and Mosiah before us, the type points to the last days when the righteous who will not take up the sword against their neighbors will have to flee to Zion for refuge.

Zeniff lived in tenuous happiness with his people in Nephi for twenty-two years. The Lamanites were a peril, but not the peril the people faced when the kingdom was passed to Zeniff's son Noah. Kingdoms fall not so often to threats from without as to spiritual rot from within. A riotous man with many wives and concubines and a passion for wine-bibbing, Noah laid a tax "of one fifth part of all they possessed"[104] upon the people to support his opulent life-style. He put down the priests of his father and consecrated new ones, ornamenting seats of pure gold for them in the temple—perhaps the one Nephi had built with such love. From this lofty place, they spoke "lying and vain words to [the] people,"[105] leading the population astray under the pretext of religion. Who could accuse them of blasphemy, idolatry, and whoredom when they followed their traditional religious forms?

The Lord sent a prophet, Abinadi, to warn Noah and his people that they would be delivered to their enemies unless they repented. Because of their iniquities, their generation would be brought into bondage, smitten on the cheek, driven by men, and eaten by wild beasts. Bondage is the natural consequence of moral slackness and degeneration, not just something superimposed by the Lord. The priests in their fine garb and self-righteousness were infuriated: "O king, what great evil hast thou done, or what great sins have thy people committed, that we should be condemned of God or judged of this man?"[106] It is usually the wicked who most vehemently cling to their beautiful self-image.

Counseling together as the Pharisees would later on another continent about Christ, the priests questioned Abinadi to trap him in his words. Quoting from Isaiah they asked as if they represented God, "What meaneth the words . . . How beautiful upon the mountains are the feet of him that bringeth good tidings?"[107] Abinadi answered, "Are you priests, and pretend to teach this people . . . and yet desire to know of me what these things mean?"[108]

Then he told them, not mincing a word. He first quoted the ten commandments and then proclaimed that "salvation doth not come by the law alone" but through the atonement "which God himself shall make."[109] "All the prophets who have prophesied ever since the world began—have they not spoken more or less concerning these things?"[110]

His words stung the priests, whose claim to power probably came from a pretense of superior knowledge, and they came to grab Abinadi. "Touch me not," he said, "for God shall smite you if ye lay your hands upon me [until I have delivered my message]."[111] His face shone even as Moses' did on Sinai, and he spoke movingly, poignantly of Christ who would break the bands of death, satisfy the demands of justice, bear our griefs, and carry our sorrows. When Abinadi had finished his message, Noah and his priests took him and burned him to death.

Even as the flames scorched his flesh, he delivered a prophecy: "Even as ye have done unto me, so shall it come to pass . . . that many shall suffer . . . even the pains of death by fire."[112]

Pages 92–93: Looking to the north across ruins at Mixco Viejo in Guatemala toward hills where ruins have also been discovered. This is much like the description of the view from Nephi of Shemlon and Shilom in the Book of Mormon. The description of Noah's ambitious building program talks not only of "many elegant and spacious buildings,"[113] a spacious palace, and a complete refurbishment of the temple, but also of a tower in Nephi that overlooked the lands of Shilom and Shemlon, and a "great tower . . . built on

the hill north of the land Shilom, which had been a resort for the children of Nephi at the time they fled out of the land."[114]

Above: Beautiful waters of Champay in Guatemalan jungle typify the waters of Mormon where Alma and the believers resorted to learn about "repentance, and redemption, and faith on the Lord,"[115] and the covenant of baptism. Though the waters of Mormon have not been discovered, clues abound in the record. The place was higher in elevation than the city of Nephi

and graced by a fountain (likely a spring) of pure water. A thicket of small trees stood by the fountain (indicating that the land otherwise might have been dry). A forest was nearby. In some seasons the land was infested by wild beasts. Alma, unlike Noah, taught the priests "not to depend upon the people for their support; but for their labor they were to receive the grace of God, that they might wax strong in the Spirit, having the knowledge of God, that they might teach with power and authority from God."[116]

binadi's mission by most worldly standards was a failure. As far as is known, of all those who listened, only one believed—but what a one. Abinadi's sole convert, Alma, would change the entire history of the Nephite people. Who, then, at any point can count their work a loss or say their works given at great cost were all in vain?

Alma, a young priest in Noah's court, first pled for Abinadi's life and then, threatened himself, fled and hid for many days, writing all that Abinadi had spoken. In the satanic darkness of Noah's court, who could have known that one small ember had been waiting to burst into flame? Repenting of his sins and hiding from the king, Alma secretly went about preaching to the people, and many believed, gathering to a fountain of pure water in the borders of the land. The wilderness plays a vital role in the Book of Mormon as a place where dissident minorities flee. Even when cities became heavily populated, vast tracts of wilderness separated them, and, true to their Bedouin heritage, the people seem to have had tents and provisions so they could leave settled areas with little notice.

At the waters of Mormon, two hundred and four souls gathered, and, having authority, Alma baptized them. Baptism signified that they were "willing to bear one another's burdens, that they may be light; yea, and are willing to mourn with those that mourn; yea, and comfort those that stand in need of comfort, and to stand as witnesses of God at all times and in all things, and in all places."[117] This teaching could not be more directly opposite from the philosophies of Noah, under which people were trodden down to elevate him, families under his tax burden were caused to mourn, and witnesses of God were burned.

The Lord's society is classless, for inequality breeds a host of miseries. The Lord commanded Alma's people "that they should look forward with one eye, having one faith and one baptism, having their hearts knit together in unity and in love one towards another."[118] Among them were no rich, but they had all things in common, imparting of their abundance to those who had but little.

It was a taste of Zion there at the waters of Mormon, at the peaceful forest of Mormon, and "how beautiful are they to the eyes of them who there came to the knowledge of their Redeemer."[119]

Water lilies grow abundantly in the lagoons and waters of the jungles of Central America. It is not known if Alma received his authority through angelic messengers or if perhaps during the three days of Abinadi's imprisonment, Alma crept into the dungeon by night and, in some quiet session with the prophet, received the priesthood and keys. The record is clear that he was authorized by the Lord to move forward in establishing the church of Christ among the believers, and that Alma, "having authority from God, ordained priests; even one priest to every fifty of their number."[120] When Alma and Helam and the other believers fled from the army of King Noah, there would have been nine priests to help with the growing flock of four hundred fifty souls.[121]

Above: King Limhi sent forty-three of his people from Nephi to find Zarahemla. They became lost and found instead a land covered with the dry bones of the Jaredites. At the La Venta Museum in Mexico is this stela, which dates to 1200–600 B.C. "The lines flowing from the back of the individual's head represented sun rays— suggesting that the first settlers came from the west. . . . The footprints suggest that the people traveled great distances. . . . The sculpture's giant sea monster . . . suggests that the people crossed the ocean."[122] The Jaredite barges are described thus: "No monster of the sea could break them."[123]

Right: West side of ancient Mixco Viejo where a narrow pass leads into the wilderness. For three generations the people of Zeniff had occupied the city of Nephi. Then, under bondage, Gideon suggested they escape through "the back pass, through the back wall, on the back side of the city."[124] In Near Eastern thinking, front is east, and back is west. Limhi's people, then, likely escaped through the west pass.

Alma's group swelled to 450 and, apprised that Noah had sent an army to look for them, "they took their tents and their families and departed into the wilderness"[125] to a valley they named Helam. Meanwhile, Noah's kingdom was disintegrating, and at the very moment when one citizen Gideon had cornered the king on a tower and was about to slay him, the king looked out and saw that the Lamanites were within the borders of the land. Noah fled with his people, but the Lamanites overtook them. In abject cowardice, he persuaded the priests and many of the men to abandon their wives and children and run. Later, in shame at leaving their families defenseless, the men turned on Noah and burned him to death, exactly as Abinadi had prophesied.

Back in the land of Nephi, Noah's son Limhi and the others who had stayed with their families became captives of the Lamanites, who demanded a tribute of half of all they possessed and "would smite them on their cheeks, and exercise authority over them."[126] It was grinding misery, bondage to their enemies, causing them to "humble themselves even to the dust."[127]

In Helam, Alma's people did not fare much better. At first prosperous and happy, they were found by Noah's priests and some Lamanites who were looking for the land of Nephi. From such events we get the sense that trade routes between areas were not well established at this period and that the terrain was complex enough that whole groups could disappear, probably through mountain passes into hidden valleys. Not far from home, groups quickly became lost wanderers.

Since Alma's people were few, they were easily dominated by the priests headed by Amulon. Amulon had an extra itch to persecute Alma because he had known him from Noah's court and was yet "wroth with him"[128] for believing the words of Abinadi. Amulon put tasks on the people and commanded them that "whosoever should be found calling upon God should be put to death."[129] Still, the people poured out their hearts to God, and He answered, "I will also ease the burdens which are put upon your shoulders, that even you cannot feel them upon your backs, even while you are in bondage . . . that ye may know of a surety that I, the Lord God, do visit my people in their afflictions.[130]

Light plays through the thick clouds in one of the corridors of travel used by the ancient Maya, and possibly by the Nephites and Lamanites, in Guatemala, just a few miles out of Coban. The account of the forty-three-person expedition that tried to find Zarahemla gives us some idea of the scale of the lands covered in the Book of Mormon. We know they came from Nephi in the south and that the land covered with bones was far in the land northward, "in a land among many waters."[131] This expedition was lost in the wilderness "for the space of many days."[132] Yet if they came from Mesoamerica, and the land of Cumorah they visited was in western New York state, their journey would have been a round trip of thousands of miles, crossing the great Mexican Desert twice as well as numerous major rivers—including the Mississippi—and lasting likely many months if not more than a year. This journey seems unlikely, which suggests a more compressed view of the geography of the Book of Mormon.

Both Alma's and Limhi's groups were in bondage, feeling the burdens and taxes of the taskmaster. How pointed, then, that of all the events from a thousand years of Nephite history, their stories are told in some detail, back-to-back. It is as if Mormon, who could not write a hundredth part of Nephite history, is trying to get our attention. In mortality, nearly all of us are in some sort of bondage—bondage of guilt, fear, debt, sin, or insecurity; we may suffer from unfulfilled expectations, poor health, or indecision over life's choices. We may feel grief over an absent loved one or despair over a weakness. Bondage comes not only from a tyrant shaking a fist over our heads. It comes as a shadow over the soul that mars our peace. How do we escape? Only the Lord offers freedom.

"I will covenant with my people and deliver them out of bondage,"[133] said the Lord, and "none could deliver them except it were the Lord their God."[134] A repentant Limhi and his people escaped out the back door of the land of Nephi while the Lamanites were in

a drunken stupor. For his part, Alma and his people escaped when the Lord caused "a deep sleep to come upon the Lamanites."[135] As our eyes are made single toward Him, He will deliver us, too. Even His commandments are but a description of how to live in a way that is not painful and imprisoning.

Both Limhi's and Alma's groups made their way back to Zarahemla to a joyous reunion where the church was organized. Limhi had tried before to find Zarahemla, sending forty-three of his people north into the wilderness to look for the city. They had become lost, however, and found instead a land covered with human bones and the ruins of buildings. They also found twenty-four gold plates presumably containing a record of a fallen people. At last, being led back to Zarahemla, Limhi brought the mysterious twenty-four plates with them, hoping King Mosiah could translate them with the Urim and Thummim. It had been eighty years and three generations since Zeniff had first left.

3

TO SING THE SONG OF REDEEMING LOVE

The church in Zarahemla began to be persecuted by the unbelievers, and among the most destructive and influential of the lot were Alma's son Alma and the four sons of Mosiah. It is tempting to read the record merely as a description of youthful rebellion, of spoiled children who wanted to pique their parents, but a careful analysis suggests something different. The elder Alma died at the age of eighty-two, between one and nine years after Alma the younger's conversion. Thus, Alma the younger may have been in his forties. Thus, he was probably a serious, sophisticated, long-term sinner who wreaked havoc with the church, "stealing away the hearts of the people" and "giving a chance for the enemy of God to exercise his power over them."[1] Who could calculate the damage he had done? And all five of these men had attacked the very thing their parents most cherished.

Alma the elder, the great high priest of the church, had prayed for his son, not just for a few months but for years, pleading with love that his blasphemous, menacing namesake might be brought to a knowledge of the truth. Then one day as Alma the younger and the sons of Mosiah were "going about rebelling against God,"[2] an angel descended in a cloud, speaking with the voice of thunder and shaking the earth on which they stood. "Why persecutest thou the church of God?"[3] he asked, and all of them fell to the earth with astonishment, recognizing the power of the Lord.

Alma was struck with such fear and amazement that for three days and nights[4] he was dumb, so that he could not open his mouth, and weak, so that he could not move. He later described his experience during that time: "I was racked with eternal torment, for my soul was harrowed up to the greatest degree and racked with all my sins. . . . I saw that I had rebelled against my God . . . and I had murdered many of his children, or rather led them away unto destruction; yea, and in fine so great had been my iniquities, that the very thought of coming into the presence of my God did rack my soul with inexpressible horror."[5]

In that moment feeling the pains of a damned soul, while his father fasted over his bedside, Alma said, "I remembered also to have heard my father prophesy unto the people concerning the coming of one Jesus Christ, a Son of God, to atone for the sins of the world."[6]

Pages 100–101: Last touches of evening light rim the mountains of the largest tributary of the Usumacinta River. From the internal clues of the Book of Mormon it is clear that the river Sidon was a north-flowing river, a major obstacle to travel, that flowed from mountainous regions into the sea. Only two major rivers in Central America fit this description, the Grijalva and the Usumacinta.

Left: Morning light begins to burn through mists and reveal trees at a valley just a few miles south of Coban, Guatemala. It seems from the record that any tributary that flowed into the river Sidon was also called Sidon. In modern times every in-flowing source has a separate name.

Above: Illuminated jungle ferns at a Guatemalan nature preserve. The constant and faithful prayers of Alma the elder for his son are telling of the efficacy of prayer. "He has prayed with much faith concerning thee," the angel said to Alma the younger about his father.[7]

Late afternoon light hits the shores of the upper reaches of the Usumacinta river in Guatemala. The river is a startling deep green. Surprisingly, the Hebrew root of Sidon is sid, meaning "lime." It may be more than coincidence that this river flows over limestone and is the color of a lime. The people of Mulek probably navigated southward along the Sidon river, finally finding an area to settle. They called their new home Zarahemla, after their leader. Some evidence suggests that Mulek, the son of Zedekiah, king of Judah, may have been taken out of Jerusalem when he was a small child and brought to this new land while still very young. The name Mulek means "little king."

In chapter 36 of the book named for him, Alma described his conversion in an ancient form of Hebrew poetry called chiasmus. In a chiasmus the first line is very like the last, the second line is like the second to the last, and so on. All the lines ultimately point to the middle of the piece, where the central meaning of the poem is stated. Remembering his father's teachings of the atonement, and feeling a pain so tormenting that he wished for banishment, he cried out, "Thou Son of God, have mercy on me, who am in the gall of bitterness, and am encircled about by the everlasting chains of death."[8] This, then, is the center of Alma's message, the center of the gospel, the center of reality from which all else flows.

In that instant, he could feel his pain no more and was no longer harrowed up by the memory of his sins: "What joy, and what marvelous light I did behold; yea, my soul was filled with joy as exceeding as was my my pain! . . . There could be nothing so exquisite and so bitter as were my pains . . . and . . . on the other hand, there can be nothing so exquisite and sweet as was my joy."[9]

This practiced sinner, who could not undo the wrong he had done, was healed by an atonement so powerful that it could descend even to one as low as he. No matter what our sin or anguish or pain, surely, then, this atonement can heal us too, making us whole, new, our past forgotten.

From that time on, Alma the younger and the sons of Mosiah went about "zealously striving to repair all the injuries they had done to the church, confessing all their sins."[10] In fact, the sons of Mosiah became filled with a desire to go preach to the Lamanites, to move into enemy territory where their lives were valued like flies on a wall. But, having endured the misery of sin, "they could not bear that any human soul should perish; yea, even the very thoughts that any soul should endure endless torment did cause them to quake and tremble."[11] It is noteworthy how much of the important work of the Book of Mormon is accomplished by the vilest sinners who have repented.

With his sons gone, King Mosiah had no one on whom to confer the kingdom. Thus, he proposed a change in the system of government from kings to judges that would be chosen by the voice of the people. Alma the younger was appointed to be the first chief judge and the high priest over the church.

Beautiful water flowers grow in abundance in the lakes, lagoons, and rivers of Guatemala. Perhaps the greatest hallmark of the nearly 33-year reign of Mosiah, son of Benjamin, was the translation of the 24 plates of Ether found by the people of Limhi. These were likely not 24 individual gold pages but rather 24 sets of large plates covering the history of the Jaredites from as early as 3000 B.C. until their destruction between 600 and 300 B.C. Mosiah was a seer, and he translated the records which were possibly written in the Adamic tongue (the language of Adam) "by the means of those two stones which were fastened into the two rims of a bow."[12] This Urim and Thummim were given to the brother of Jared on the mount Shelem.[13]

Above: Ornate stela (circa A.D. 700) at Quirigua in eastern Guatemala. Costly apparel is a mark of pride in the Book of Mormon. The people of the Lord "did impart of their substance . . . to the poor, and the needy, and the sick, and the afflicted; and they did not wear costly apparel, yet they were neat and comely."[14] The people of the world wore "costly apparel; being lifted up in the pride of their own eyes."[15]

Right: Jungle trail in the Lachua Reserve in northern Guatemala may look similar to ancient trails cut by the Nephites. Wicked Amlici is never mentioned as being a Nephite and may have been a descendent of Zarahemla, believing that by birthright he should rule. Many of the battles of the Book of Mormon probably came from contending lineages, each claiming the throne. Amlici's motive was power, and his appeal was intellectual. But, "it is not common that the voice of the people desireth anything contrary to that which is right," but "if the time comes that the voice of the people doth choose iniquity . . . then is the time [God] will visit you with great destruction."[16]

Alma was chief judge for nine years, during which time he had to face civil war as one Amlici made a bid to be king, and, losing, enlisted the Lamanites to join with him in an all-out battle for the throne. Yet a more grievous problem to Alma was that the people of the church "began to wax proud, because of their exceeding riches . . . and . . . they began to wear very costly apparel."[17] Among them "were envyings, and strife, and malice, and persecutions."[18] Worldly power has no pull for the godly. Others may lie, cheat, and steal for it, but the good leaders of the Book of Mormon readily drop positions of power to do the more important work of "bearing down in pure testimony"[19] toward their wandering neighbors. The world seeks to change people from the outside with a new program, a new coercion, a new law. The Lord works from the inside, changing the human soul; then all else changes.

So Alma didn't look back as he relinquished his judgeship in its ninth year and began traveling throughout the land from one city to the next teaching the gospel. He began in Zarahemla, speaking from intense personal experience: "Have ye spiritually been born of God? Have ye received his image in your countenances? Have ye experienced this mighty change in your hearts?"[20] What he was asking was not outward conformity to law, the superficial patina of spirituality, but a change in their very natures, altering the state of their hearts, their way of perceiving themselves and the universe. This was not to be achieved in a single moment with a simple acceptance of Christ. Rather, it was a process. The natural man is overcome not just by gritting one's teeth and trying hard for self-improvement but ultimately by being transformed through the power of the Holy Ghost.

If the natural man grabs for things, believing he must fend for himself, one born of the Spirit trusts in the Lord with all his heart. If the natural man sees others as competitors, one born of the Spirit sees others as brothers and sisters. If the natural man feels he must create a good impression, never admitting error, one born again knows he must grow line upon line. Alma said, "If ye have experienced a change of heart, and if ye have felt to sing the song of redeeming love, I would ask, can ye feel so now?"[21]

From Zarahemla, Alma traveled to Gideon, Melek, and finally Ammonihah, where he was reviled, spat upon, and finally in humiliation thrown out. Journeying away from the city and weighed down with sorrow for the sins of the people, Alma beheld an angel, who said, "Lift up thy head and rejoice . . . for thou hast been faithful in keeping the commandments of God from the time which thou receivedst thy first message from him. Behold, I am he that delivered it unto you."[22] The angel said to go back to Ammonihah, and without hesitation Alma "returned speedily."[23] Like Peter, who "straightway"[24] left his fishing nets, and Nephi, who immediately arose and went up to the mountain, the faithful respond to the Lord's most difficult requests with complete submission.

As He always does, the Lord had prepared a way for the fasting, exhausted Alma. Upon his return to the city, he met Amulek, an influential man who had been visited by the same angel and told that he would feed and bless a holy man. For several days, Alma rested and taught Amulek; then together they faced the city.

Ammonihah was arrogant and conceited, the foundation of her destruction laid by the unrighteousness of her lawyers and judges who stirred up the people to riotings and disturbances that they might get more money in suits. When Alma warned them they were ripe for destruction because they had chosen iniquity, they scoffed, not knowing the power of God: "We will not believe thy words if thou shouldst prophesy that this great city should be destroyed in one day."[25] Unbeknownst to them, these were foreshadowing words.

Then lying Zeezrom stepped forth, hoping to catch Amulek in his words and offering a small fortune, six onties of silver, if he would deny the existence of God. Alma and Amulek were not to be snared in the trap and taught him instead the plan of salvation. All shall be resurrected, they said, "both old and young, both bond and free, both male and female, both the wicked and the righteous; and even there shall not so much as a hair of their heads be lost; but every thing shall be restored to its perfect frame."[26] As they preached, Zeezrom became silent and began trembling under the consciousness of his own guilt.

When "the spirit and the body shall be reunited again in its perfect form," the time shall come when "we shall be brought to stand before God, knowing even as we know now, and have a bright recollection of all our guilt,"[27] Amulek taught his fellow citizens. Since mortal life is a time of probation, if we have not repented, our words, works, and thoughts will condemn us, and "in this awful state we shall not dare to look up to our God."[28]

Yet the plan of salvation has been designed from the beginning to spare us from this condemning moment. Just as Christ spared all of us from the permanent effects of physical death, through His atoning sacrifice He will spare the repentant from spiritual death. This life, not some other more convenient time, is the time to prepare to meet God.

Alma told the gathered crowd that many had been especially ordained to teach this message. They were "called and prepared from the foundation of the world according to the foreknowledge of God, on account of their exceeding faith and good works."[29]

Pages 108–9: Post-classic Temple of the Cross at Palenque in Tabasco, Mexico. Zeezrom repented and became a great missionary. It is better to stay on the strait and narrow path, but we can take hope in the fact that some of the vilest sinners (Alma the elder, Alma the younger, Ammon, Aaron, Omner, Himni, Zeezrom, Lamoni, Lamoni's father, the Anti-Nephi-Lehies, Amulek and Corianton) became some of the greatest missionaries of all time.

Left: Vultures are common in Mesoamerica. A vulture's tremendous sense of smell can lead it to carrion miles away. Lawyercraft was big business in Ammonihah. Joseph Smith spoke of "priest-craft, lawyer-craft, and doctor-craft" with disdain.[30]

Above: Plaza of the Lost World in Tikal. The Book of Mormon paints a picture of loosely connected city-states with slow communications between them. Without a central church administration, Alma, and later Nephi and Helaman, traveled from city to city setting the church in order.

To Alma's and Amulek's outspoken words, some repented, believed, and searched the scriptures, but Zeezrom was "harrowed up"[31] in guilty remorse and tried to take back his words. His townsfolk spat on him and cast him out, then turned their fury on Alma and Amulek and the believers still in the city.

Gathering the believers, they threw them into a fire with their holy scriptures and brought Alma and Amulek to watch. Seeing the pain of the women and children being consumed in the fire, Amulek cried, "How can we witness this awful scene? Therefore let us stretch forth our hands, and exercise the power of God which is in us, and save them from the flames."[32] We know that Amulek's father and kinsfolk were alive after the conflagration, but his wife and children are mentioned only before. One wonders if he might have been watching the burning of part of his family. This is further suggested because after they left Ammonihah, Alma took a distraught Amulek to his own home, where he "did administer unto him in his tribulations, and strengthened him in the Lord."[33]

Yet, while the believers burned, Alma and Amulek watched helplessly because the Spirit constrained them to not stretch forth their hands and with the power of God stop it. Thus, the "blood of the innocent [would] stand as a witness"[34] against the people of Ammonihah. Then Alma and Amulek were thrown in prison, where those of the religion of Nehor gnashed their teeth and spat upon them. At issue for the Nehors was not just religious but also political power, for the two are inextricably linked in the record.

After days of hunger and thirst, surrounded by mockers, Alma arose and cried, "How long shall we suffer these great afflictions, O Lord? O Lord, give us strength according to our faith which is in Christ, even unto deliverance."[35] Suddenly the cords with which they were bound broke, the earth shook, and the prison walls fell to the earth, killing all who had mocked them. The others fled in fear "from the presence of Alma and Amulek even as a goat fleeth with her young from two lions."[36] These prison walls are another tangible type repeated so often in the record that we are not to miss it. We are in bondage until Christ releases us.

113

Pages 112–13: The road that leads from modern Coban to Lanquin is graced by spectacular scenery. The people of Ammonihah were destroyed by the Lamanites in a terrible battle. Ammonihah becomes a type to take note of—a city, state, or nation convinced of its greatness, and completely turned from the Lord, becomes a prime candidate for destruction.

Above: Horses are mentioned throughout the Book of Mormon until A.D. 26. Were these horses like this horse in the upper cloud forest of Guatemala? For years archaeologists have doubted that horses existed in Mesoamerica before the time of Columbus, using the mention of them to point to the Book of Mormon's inauthenticity. This view, however, is changing as "actual horse bones have been found in a number of archaeological sites on the Yucatan Peninsula, in one case with artifacts six feet beneath the surface under circumstances that rule out their coming from Spanish horses."[37] Some feel that the word horse *in the Book of Mormon is used to refer to a deer or some other domesticated animal.*

Just before Alma became chief judge, the sons of Mosiah and their party went south to the Lamanites with missionary fervor and the sense that "great was the work which they had undertaken."[38] They went to a wild, hardened, and ferocious people "who delighted in murdering"[39] Nephites, yet their father, King Mosiah, had obtained a promise from the Lord that his sons would be delivered. At a crossroads, with blessings and good-byes, the group separated, "every man alone."[40] Events that follow show us that Mosiah's son Ammon was the mightiest warrior of the Nephites, "to whom no man or platoon of men [could] stand up."[41] He could have dealt with his enemy by wading in and cleaning the place up, but instead in the next fourteen years he and his brothers traveled from house to house, "patiently suffering every privation, 'relying upon the mercies of God,' teaching the people in their houses and in their streets, being 'cast out, and mocked, and spit upon, and smote upon [their] cheeks,' "[42] hoping to save just one soul. And, according to the Lord, "that is the way you deal with the bad guys."[43] Enemies become friends who bury their weapons.

It began for Ammon in the land of Ishmael, where, bearing the old hatreds, it was the people's "custom to bind all the Nephites who fell into their hands"[44] and carry them to their king, Lamoni. Before the Lamanite king, here was the son of the Nephite king, himself in line for the throne. Remarkably, Ammon volunteered to be the king's servant and was given a job watching the flocks. Why did Ammon put up with all this? Because the Lord had promised, "I will make an instrument of thee in my hands unto the salvation of many souls," and he knew it was better to be an instrument for the Lord than to rule as the mightiest king.

Lamanites from a good-sized area drove their flocks to Sebus to water, suggesting that the land here was dry. At any rate, they made an ongoing sport of scattering the king's flocks. Like the Bedouins from whom they sprang, their creed seemed to be, "As long as we live we shall plunder and raid."[45] The king's servants wept when their flocks were scattered because they knew their master would kill them, but Ammon saw it as a chance to show the power of the Lord. Gathering their flocks again, the servants

encircled them, while Ammon stood to meet the wave of attacking men. The Lamanites did not know that by however many they outnumbered this one warrior, they could never slay him. Why? Because the Lord had promised Mosiah that He would protect his sons. "What I the Lord have spoken, I have spoken, and I excuse not myself."[46] Unlike mortals, the Lord always keeps His word.

A battle of swords and slings followed. Ammon smote off the arm of every man who raised his sword against him, and then the servants carried these arms back to the king as a testimony of Ammon's might. That any one man should have such power in battle dumbfounded the king, and he was further amazed when, calling for Ammon, he found that he was out preparing the king's horses and chariot as he had earlier been asked. Had the king ever before seen anyone so powerful and faithful? The king said, "Now I surely know that this is the Great Spirit."[47] He called Ammon before him but sat silent for an hour, too overwhelmed to speak.

Light shimmers upon the waters of the Motagua River, which runs west to east across Guatemala. In an area that may have been like this one, south of the narrow strip of wilderness, the Lamanites lived and had their cities. In the dry season, when the surrounding countryside is parched, flocks would have to be driven to a central area for watering. The record suggests this type of setting as the servants of Lamoni went "forth with their flocks to the place of water, which was called the water of Sebus, and all the Lamanites drive their flocks hither, that they may have water."[48] After 200 B.C. the Nephites tended to live in the wet lowlands, while the Lamanites tended to live in the highlands with distinct wet and dry seasons.

Ammon broke the silence by teaching Lamoni about the source of his marvelous power. "Believest thou that there is a God? . . . Yea, and he looketh down upon all the children of men; and he knows all the thoughts and intents of the heart; for by his hand were they all created from the beginning."[49] The fierce Lamoni had been made ready to listen, and Ammon taught him, starting from the creation, the plan of redemption. Believing, Lamoni cried out, "O Lord, have mercy . . . upon me"[50] and then fell to the earth as if he were dead.

Two days and nights passed with Lamoni unmoving. Many were ready to put his body into a sepulchre, but the queen first wanted Ammon's opinion. Ammon knew that "the dark veil of unbelief was being cast away from his mind," and that he was infused with such light that it "had overcome his natural frame, and he was carried away in God."[51] So, turning away those who would bury him, the queen watched over his bed through the night. The next day Lamoni arose, solemnly declaring that he had seen his Redeemer. Then, his heart swollen with joy, he and the queen and Ammon all sank to the earth, overpowered by the Spirit.

Seeing this and fearing God, the king's servants fell to the earth as well, crying unto the Lord. Abish, a Lamanite woman, "having been converted unto the Lord for many years, on account of a remarkable vision of her father,"[52] looked at all the fallen bodies around her and, recognizing the power of God in the event, went from house to house, calling the people to come. As they thronged the palace, they contended. Ammon was the Great Spirit, said some; he had been sent by the Great Spirit to afflict them, said others. But as Lamoni and the others arose, they all declared "the self-same thing—that their hearts had been changed; that they had no more desire to do evil."[53] As many as believed on their words were baptized, and a church was established among them.

Soon after, the Lord told Ammon that his brethren were in prison in Middoni and that He should deliver them. On the journey there, Ammon and Lamoni met Lamoni's father, the king of all the land, who asked with fury, "Whither art thou going with this Nephite, who is one of the children of a liar?"[54]

Enraged, Lamoni's father drew his sword first to slay his son, and, then thinking better of it, turned his sword on Ammon, but no one could beat this warrior of God. When the king saw that Ammon could kill him, he pled, "If thou wilt spare me I will grant unto thee whatsoever thou wilt ask, even to half of the kingdom."[55] Ammon, however, wanted nothing for himself, only the king's guarantee that his brothers could be freed from prison and that Lamoni could retain his kingdom.

Long after that moment, the incident still haunted the king. In fact, when Ammon's brother Aaron, now released from prison, visited him in his palace, he offered to be his servant, but the king refused. All he wanted was to be taught, for, he said, "I have been somewhat troubled in mind because of the generosity and the greatness of the words of thy brother Ammon."[56] It was not the power of the sword that had stayed with the king but the power of love and sacrifice, the most awesome power in the universe, piercing even the ferocious old tyrant's heart.

Aaron expounded the gospel, and the king asked, "What shall I do that I may have this eternal life of which thou hast spoken?" Aaron answered that he should repent of his sins and "bow down before God, and call on his name in faith."[57] The crusty, arrogant ruler responded with one of the most yearning prayers in the Book of Mormon. Prostrating himself upon the ground, he cried, "O God, Aaron hath told me that there is a God; and if there is a God, and if thou art God, wilt thou make thyself known unto me, and *I will give away all my sins to know thee*."[58] What he offered was exactly what is required. We may be content to be simply nice people, good enough, holding on here and there to our most comfortable and familiar sins. Many of those sins we have lived with so long that they feel like a part of us, our way of seeing things, even our security. The specific sins—the angry snap at a child, the critical judgment of another—are but manifestations of the sinfulness still a part of our nature. It is, then, pieces of our very nature that we have to give up, painfully letting part of ourselves die—the natural man—but it is well worth the sacrifice. What the Lord wants of His children is not simply to be nice people but also to be mirrors of Himself, full of "such energy and joy and wisdom and love as we cannot now imagine."[59]

Pages 116–17: The 10,000-foot-high Cuchumatanes in Guatemala, a candidate for the narrow strip of wilderness. The remarkable mission of Ammon, Aaron, Omner, Himni and their brethren south of this strip to the Lamanites converted a people who "never did fall away."[60]

Left: Swinging bridge of the modern Mayan Indians dangles above the Selegua River in Guatemala. Crossings similar to this were used anciently. Of all the rivers, ravines, canyons, or seas to cross, however, one stands above all, and the Lord "in his great mercy hath brought us over that everlasting gulf of death and misery, even to the salvation of our souls."[61]

Above: Thirsty grounds of the Guatemalan highlands are criss-crossed with trails of flocks and herds in the dry season. Travel in the Book of Mormon is consistently marked by rapid movement along east-to-west paths and difficult, slow movement along north-and-south paths.

119

With the king of the Lamanites and all his household converted, a new decree was sent throughout the land that the four sons of Mosiah and their brethren should not be stoned, scourged, spat upon, or thrown out of synagogues but rather allowed to preach freely. The ancient hatred toward the Nephites was miraculously cast aside as thousands laid down their weapons of war, their well-trained impulses to fight, and were brought to believe in the Lord. To signify their new life, they took a new name, no longer wishing to be called Lamanites but instead Anti-Nephi-Lehies, meaning "like unto Nephi of old."

With sore hatred, and no doubt feeling politically threatened, the unbelieving Lamanites made preparations for war against the Anti-Nephi-Lehies. Born to war, no group was better able to defend themselves, but as they counseled together, not one of the believers was willing to take up arms against their brethren. Their king, calling the believers tenderly "my best beloved brethren," put it this way: "Since it has been all that we could do (as we were the most lost of all mankind), to repent of all our sins and the many murders which we have committed, and to get God to take them away from our hearts . . . let us stain our swords no more with the blood of our brethren . . . for perhaps, if we should stain our swords again they can no more be washed bright through the blood of the Son of our great God."[62]

When the king had finished talking, the people dug a hole in the earth, and together they took their weapons, the slashing, beating, skull-crushing weapons for shedding blood, and buried them with a covenant to God "that rather than shed the blood of their brethren they would give up their own lives."[63]

Has there been a more committed, courageous people? Did they look at their children and spouses with tears as the Lamanite army thundered toward them? "They went out to meet them, and prostrated themselves before them to the earth, and began to call on the name of the Lord; and thus they were in this attitude when the Lamanites began to fall upon them, and began to slay them with the sword."[64]

More than a thousand of the Anti-Nephi-Lehies were slaughtered as they lay calling upon their God. Seeing this pitiful sight, more than that number in the attacking army threw down their weapons, their hearts swollen with shame. But many of the other warriors, hardened by war, responded differently. Stung that they had slain their own brethren, they took out their hot anger by crossing into the land of Zarahemla and destroying the wicked Nephite city Ammonihah in a single day. Surely, somewhere in the wasted city, the words still echoed with which they had once taunted Alma: "We will not believe thy words if thou shouldst prophesy that this great city should be destroyed in one day."[65]

As Lamanite aggressions spread, the defenseless Anti-Nephi-Lehies were in unbearable danger. Finally, deciding to seek refuge with the Nephites, they said in a spirit of meekness, "we will go down unto our brethren, and we will be their slaves until we repair unto them the many murders and sins which we have committed against them."[66] Ammon marveled at the utterly transforming power of the atonement, "If we had not come up out of the land of Zarahemla, these our dearly beloved brethren, who have so dearly beloved us, would still have been racked with hatred against us, yea, and they would also have been strangers to God."[67]

Directed by the Lord, Ammon and his brothers began moving the Anti-Nephi-Lehies to the safety of Zarahemla. On their journey, to their astonishment, they came upon their old friend Alma, whom they had neither seen nor heard from for fourteen years. Ammon's happiness was so great that he was "swallowed up in the joy of his God."[68] What added most to Alma's joy was that Mosiah's sons "were still his brethren in the Lord," and they had "taught with power and authority of God."[69] Together they asked the Nephite chief judge to send a proclamation throughout the land, desiring the voice of the people on admitting the Anti-Nephi-Lehies. An affirmative word was returned, and Alma and Ammon went back to the wilderness where the believers had pitched their tents, anxiously waiting for the word. Would they be accepted?

It must have been a tender meeting. Alma told his conversion story. All of these had once been heinous sinners; all were now a pure people through Jesus Christ.

Pages 120–21: Evening light brightly beams in eastern Guatemala just south of the country of Belize. The land of Jershon, where the people of Ammon settled, was located by the sea, due east of the land of Zarahemla. The little children may have watched as their fathers covenanted with the Lord to bury their weapons and never take them up again. It is poignant that soon thereafter 1,005 of these covenant-makers were slain. These young children, many raised fatherless, became the mighty 2,060 warriors of Helaman and would have such powerful faith in what their mothers had taught them that not one would be slain in battle.

Left: Beautiful golden wheat, stacked and ready for the threshing floor, is harvested by hand in the mountains of Guatemala. Ammon and his brethren rejoiced at the end of their fourteen-year mission among the Lamanites. "Behold," Ammon said, "the field was ripe, and blessed are ye, for ye did thrust in the sickle, and did reap with your might, yea, all the day long did ye labor; and behold the number of your sheaves!"[70]

Lest we have some question, the contrast between a righteous and a wicked society is starkly and repeatedly drawn in the Book of Mormon and stands as a measure for our own world. The Lord wants His children to be equal, imparting of their abundance to the poor so that all may be of one heart. A slick, eloquent character named Korihor came into the land of Zarahemla and voiced the principles of wickedness, making a special appeal to the beautiful people of property. "Every man," he said, "fared in this life according to the management of the creature; therefore every man prospered according to his genius, and . . . every man conquered according to his strength; and whatsoever a man did was no crime."[71]

If this argument sounds strikingly familiar, it should. It is the outlook of the secular world, giving a philosophical sanction to inequality and the misery it breeds. Life is a race, it says, where only the fit survive, and therefore whatever it takes to survive in high style is allowed. Whoever was trampled upon and left behind, bloody and exhausted, was simply not fit enough. As one writer observed, "Note well the sequence of folly: first we are well pleased with ourselves because of our wealth, then comes the game of status and prestige, leading to competitive maneuvers, hatred, and dirty tricks. . . . Where wealth guarantees respectability, principles melt away as the criminal element rises to the top. . . . It ends in utter frustration and total insecurity as morals and the market collapse together and the baffled experts surrender."[72]

Korihor knew just how to make his argument. Since there is no God, he said, then there is no sin. At death, all accounts are settled. With a superior air, he referred to the believers as bound down with "foolish ordinances" and "foolish traditions."[73] Their ancient priests sought to "keep them in ignorance."[74] Here is another pattern; the skeptics have ever called the believers naive, using the pretext that they, themselves, are the truth seekers who have just never found evidence of God. Alma caught Korihor in his own game, asking, "What evidence have ye that there is no God . . . ? I say unto you that ye have none."[75]

Pages 124–25: Looking east at ancient temples in Tikal. Apostasy turned the Book of Mormon people from simple life-styles to ostentatious patterns of building, trivializing of sacred things, committing of whoredoms, denial of prophecy and revelation, and proliferation of priestcraft. "Priestcrafts are that men preach and set themselves up for a light unto the world, that they may get gain and praise of the world."[76] Korihor was one, like Nehor, who fell into this deadly pattern.

Above: Egrets gather to fish at the narrowest point of the eastern outlet of Lago de Izabal. The land of Antionum, where the Zoramites lived, adjoined the southern part of the land of Jershon. Both were on the east near the sea. All the descriptions of travel between the two lands use the word "over," perhaps referring to a floating bridge or boat crossing. The Nephites likely would have given a land to the people of Ammon (the Anti-Nephi-Lehies) that had some sort of natural protection, such as a water barrier, to help them in their promises of military protection.

If the righteous are bonded by love to each other, nobody is so ultimately alone as the wicked. Therefore, it was no surprise that Korihor was finally trampled to death by a group as perverse as himself—the Zoramites. These Nephite dissenters lived on the eastern shores of the land in Antionum, a sort of buffer between the Lamanites on the south and the land of Jershon on the north where the Anti-Nephi-Lehies, now called the people of Ammon, had settled. Alma must have seen the dissenters as threatening, for if the Zoramites sided with the Lamanites, the people of Ammon would be exposed. Probably concerned about the threat this posed as well as the state of their souls, Alma went to Antionum with the strongest set of missionaries he could muster—three of the sons of Mosiah, Zeezrom, Amulek, and two of his own sons.

They were aghast at what they found. Alma had seen believers burned before his eyes, but no wickedness pierced him as that of the Zoramites. He cried, "O Lord, wilt thou give me strength, that I may bear with mine infirmities."[77] It was not necessarily that the Zoramites were immoral. In fact, from Alma's brief description we see that they were clearly enterprising, able, industrious, well-scrubbed, and Sabbath-day abiding. What, then, was so horrible as to make Alma's soul shrink?

The Zoramites had built a tower called the Rameumptom. On one day of the week, they strutted around in ornate costumes, then one by one climbed the tower and proclaimed, "Holy God, we believe that . . . thou hast elected us that we shall be saved, whilst all around us are elected to be cast by thy wrath down to hell . . . and again we thank thee, O God, that we are a chosen and a holy people."[78] Here was unbounded self-deceit under the guise of holiness. Self-deceit is a most dangerous condition, sponsored by the father of lies. If, like the Zoramites, to preserve our wonderful self-image we are led to hide from our own sins, we become unable to repent and instead waste our energy defending our goodness. Yet self-deceit can take another form, too. We can also see our sins yet find them so painful that for the sake of our own well-being we avoid facing them. Either approach is soul-destroying and denies our fundamental need for Jesus Christ.

Looking southeast across the rich and fertile lands of the Motagua River basin in eastern Guatemala, a candidate of some scholars for the land of Antionum. The Sierra Del Espiritu Santo range of mountains are in the background, perhaps the place where the Lamanites were living. Amazingly, just a few miles to the west of this area is dry, arid land. The Book of Mormon seems to indicate that the Zoramites who came to Antionum may have been an "expansionist elite group" who "imposed political control and their own religious cults on the less militant inhabitants; the conquered peoples thereafter maintained the elite and constructed the great ceremonial centers under their direction."[79] Hence we see the common people complaining to Alma about being cast out of the very synagogues they had built with their own hands and Alma's utter astonishment and dismay at the Zoramites' manner of worship.

The Zoramites had cast the poor from their synagogues. Outcast, in their despised state, they were ready to listen to the preaching of Alma and Amulek. From the Hill Onidah Alma began, "There are many who do say: If thou wilt show unto us a sign from heaven, then we shall know of a surety; then we shall believe."[81] Yet this is not the order of heaven. While God is a God of miracles and signs, they are not given to coerce people into belief. Such belief is transitory—momentarily compelling but fleeting once the signs that prop it up are removed.

Instead, Alma told the gathered multitude, the way they could come to believe was by planting the word of God like a seed in their hearts and nourishing it by faith. "Now, if ye give place, that a seed may be planted in your heart, behold, if it be a true seed, or a good seed, if ye do not cast it out by your unbelief . . . it will begin to swell within your breasts; and . . . ye will begin to say within yourselves—It must needs be that this is a good seed, or that the word is good, for it beginneth to enlarge my soul; yea, it beginneth to enlighten my understanding, yea, it beginneth to be delicious to me."[82]

This word of God to be planted in our hearts is the same word John referred to in his gospel: "In the beginning was the Word, and the Word was with God, and the Word was God."[83] What then is this word? Not just the gospel message but Jesus Christ Himself. We are to plant the Lord in our hearts, the center of our souls from which life flows, and let His being transform and enlarge our own. This is a far different message from obeying a set of rules imposed upon us from outside ourselves. This is, as Paul said, letting Christ be formed in us. The word, planted as a seed, grows up, of course, to be the tree of life. All the images here are of goodness, deliciousness, "most precious . . . sweet above all that is sweet."[84]

Alma then called upon these poor stragglers of Antionum to exercise faith unto repentance because God was intimately, personally interested in their happiness. The self-important Zoramites may have cast them out of the synagogue, but the Lord of all had room for them. The Zoramites may have chanted their haughty prayers and "returned to their homes, never speaking of their God again until they had assembled themselves together again,"[85] but believers prayed always over the details of their lives: "Cry unto him when ye are in your fields, yea, over all your flocks. Cry unto him in your houses, yea, over all your household, both morning, mid-day, and evening. . . . Cry unto him over the crops of your fields, that ye may prosper in them. Cry over the flocks of your fields, that they may increase. But this is not all; ye must pour out your souls in your closets, and your secret places, and in your wilderness."[86]

Still, warned Amulek, their prayers would avail them nothing if they were to "turn away the needy, and the naked, and visit not the sick and afflicted."[87] The Lord is serious about this obligation, for on it hang not only His answering of our prayers, but also, as King Benjamin told his people, the retaining of a remission of our sins. Who could have more clearly understood this teaching than those who in their poverty had been turned out?

In certain seasons the trees of the jungle begin to bloom in vibrant beauty like this one in the canyon near San Pedro Carche in Guatemala. If the Zoramites lived among beautiful trees and lush lands, the symbol of a seed being planted in their hearts should have been clear to them. That word would grow unto a mighty tree, even "a tree springing up unto everlasting life,"[88] a tree with fruit that is "pure above all that is pure; and ye shall feast upon this fruit even until ye are filled, that ye hunger not, neither shall ye thirst."[89] All these images are there to remind us of the Savior, "the Only Begotten of the Father, full of grace, and mercy, and truth."[90]

While preaching with his father in Antionum, Alma's son Corianton slipped across the border to the land of the Lamanites, enticed by the harlot Isabel. The Book of Mormon labels non-Christian religious cults as idolatrous, but Nephi refuses to tell us more, not wanting to pollute the minds of posterity. What is hinted at, however, is that Isabel and her followers are part of a nature and fertility cult that archaeology shows us was prevalent during pre-classic times in Mesoamerica, perhaps a remnant of Baal worship carried from the East. When Corianton went over to another country, he may have been with others, then, who had participated in abominable rites.[92]

At any rate, Alma was shocked and gave plain-spoken correction to his son. Not only had he damaged himself, but he had also imperiled the Zoramite mission. "When they saw your conduct they would not believe in my words,"[93] Alma told his son bluntly. "I say unto you, wickedness never was happiness."[94] The Lord's commandments are not straitjackets to bind us; they are the only way to joy. "Ye cannot hide your crimes from God,"[95] Alma said. Further, we cannot hide our crimes from ourselves, for they damage our spirits. It has been noted that "the good that one does to another is restored through the creation of peace and confidence inside himself; the evil that he does to another creates fear in himself."[96] Purity fills the disciple with spiritual confidence; wickedness, with emptiness.

Alma put it this way: "Therefore, my son, see that you are merciful unto your brethren; deal justly, judge righteously, and do good continually . . . then shall ye receive your reward; yea, ye shall have mercy . . . justice . . . a righteous judgment restored unto you again; and ye shall have good rewarded unto you again. For that which ye do send out shall return unto you again."[97] God will not make the angry heart loving nor the envious one content.

What we sow into the world, we reap in our own hearts, building spiritual confidence or disarray. Righteousness is its own reward, for it is "that same spirit which doth possess your bodies at the time that ye go out of this life . . . [that] will have power to possess your body in that eternal world."[98]

Large crocodile found commonly in the lagoons and jungles of Central America and the lands of the Book of Mormon. These crocodiles can grow to be 15 feet long and weigh nearly 500 pounds. Forty to sixty sharp teeth fill the jaws and are interlocked when closed. With the powerful muscles for closing the jaw, the crocodile can easily crush the bones of its prey, but the jaws can be kept closed with merely the strength of a human hand. Joseph Smith was told by the Lord that "if the very jaws of hell shall gape open the mouth wide after thee, know thou, my son, that all these things shall give thee experience, and shall be for thy good."[91]

Above: Rich, deep red flowers of the low-land jungle near Chisec, Guatemala, are enticing, beautiful, and deadly poisonous. Corianton's entanglements with the wicked harlot Isabel were frighteningly serious, and Alma reminded him to use forbearance: "cross yourself in all these things."[99] *It may be significant to note that "Isabel was the name of the Patroness of Harlots in the religion of the Phoenicians."*[100] *This name was likely a*

title, not a common name, with the "bel" suffix probably referring to "Baal" wor-ship and idolatry.

Pages 132–33: Shadows of clouds in afternoon light play on the fields and mountains at the modern border of Mexico, near La Mesilla, and Guatemala. While showing the sacred interpreters or Urim and Thummim to Helaman, Alma quoted the Lord, saying, "I will prepare unto my servant Gazelem, a stone, which

shall shine forth in darkness unto light."[101] *Alma was referring to the prophet Joseph Smith and the latter-day work of bringing forth the Book of Mormon. Significantly, the Lord refers personally to Joseph Smith six times in early editions of the Doctrine and Covenants as "Gazelam," which is likely a variant spelling on Gazelem and could be a title having to do with the power to translate ancient records.*[102]

The record-keepers like Alma in the Book of Mormon had a sacred sense of the importance of their mission. They felt themselves a part of an ongoing covenant lineage that God had sustained through all afflictions. For them, this stretched back in time to Abraham, Isaac, and Jacob and forward into their own hearts. Apart from Israel, they were still not apart. Thus, though Lehi's journey was 530 years earlier, Alma referred to it with a sense of personal attachment as if it were yesterday, knowing specific details of a story that must have been rehearsed to him from his youth. For him and all the Nephite prophets, this covenant sense also stretched forward into the future. They understood that through their records the Lord would "show forth his power . . . unto future generations."[103]

Thus, it was a sober moment when Alma passed the treasures of the Nephite nation to his son Helaman, explaining the significance of each one. In the cache were the plates of brass, the large and small plates of Nephi, the interpreters, the Liahona, and the sword of Laban. When Joseph Smith and Oliver Cowdery were shown the repository of Nephite records, they reportedly said that "they walked into a cave, in which there was a large and spacious room" where a large table stood. "Under this table there was a pile of plates as much as two feet high, and there were altogether in this room more plates than probably many wagonloads."[104]

Each Nephite treasure had its symbolic significance. The plates of brass had "brought them to the knowledge of the Lord their God."[105] The sword of Laban was a symbol that if the people kept the Lord's commandments, He would prosper them in the land, and that while they served Him they would not be conquered. Alma said that the twenty-four plates of Ether and the interpreters were prepared that the Lord would bring to light secret works and abominations. Finally, the Liahona, which had brought their fathers to the promised land, was like the "words of Christ, [which] if we follow their course, [will] carry us beyond this vale of sorrow into a far better land of promise."[106]

No one was a more vicious enemy to the Nephites than dissenting Nephites who joined the Lamanites. In this category was Amalickiah, a smooth-talking, base, unscrupulous man who in every way epitomizes the anti-Christ, undoubtedly the nastiest character in the Book of Mormon, made particularly dangerous because he was appealing to many. Like Satan before him, his goal was to be number one. First, he wanted to be king of the Nephites. Failing there, he took his people and departed to the Lamanites. The Lamanite king agreed to fight the Nephites with Amalickiah, but upon receiving the king's war proclamation, his people refused to fight and gathered themselves into the wilderness. Angry, the Lamanite king sent Amalickiah with an army after these rebels, but Amalickiah struck a secret deal with the rebel leader, Lehonti, to surrender the king's forces without a fight if he could become Lehonti's second in command. Then Amalickiah had poison administered by degrees to Lehonti, upon whose death he became commander of the combined Lamanite forces.

Left: Ancient trenches, extensive remains of a defensive fortification system, are still evident in valleys around Coban, Guatemala, near some of the headwaters of the Usumacinta River. This is a candidate for Manti and headwaters of the Sidon. Excavation of the trenches reveals artifacts dating to the 100 B.C. to 50 B.C. period. Manti was one of the great strongholds of the Nephites and served to protect the entrance into the land of Zarahemla.

Above: Morning light dissipates patchy fog in a valley south of Coban, Guatemala. From the detailed clues given in chapters 43 and 44 of Alma about the battle between the Nephites and the Lamanites, the battle may have taken place in this valley. We learn that the highly strategic Nephite line of defense from west to east along the narrow strip of wilderness included the cities of Antiparah and Judea near the west sea (likely the Pacific) to Moroni on the east sea (likely the Caribbean). Between them lay the highland defenses of Cumeni, Zeezrom, Manti, and Nephihah,[107] possibly protecting mountain passes.

The treachery and deceit continued. Amalickiah marched the warriors back to the Lamanite capital city, and they "bowed themselves before the king, as if to reverence him because of his greatness."[108] However, as the king put forth his hand to raise them up in a gesture of peace, he was stabbed to the heart by Amalickiah's men. Amalickiah blamed the king's servants for the assassination, married his wife, and became king of the Lamanites, a king whose dark obsession was to trample his own Nephite people.

This, then, was the venomous and cunning enemy Captain Moroni was up against in the 73 B.C. wars, which would continue for at least twelve years. Readers are meant to see that the two are complete opposites, the very essence of the Christ figure pitted against the anti-Christ.

The Nephites were taught never to take the offensive in war and never to lift their sword against an enemy unless it was to preserve their own lives and liberty. Seeing Amalickiah's designs to destroy the church and their freedom, then, Moroni rallied his countrymen: "He rent his coat; and he took a piece thereof, and wrote upon it—In memory of our God, our religion, and freedom, and our peace, our wives, and our children."[109] Calling this the title of liberty, he bowed himself to the earth and "prayed mightily unto his God for the blessings of liberty . . . so long as there should a band of Christians remain to possess the land."[110]

In essence he was calling on the covenant of the promised land, the promise of the Lord's protection for the righteous, given first to Lehi and repeated at least twenty-six times in the Book of Mormon. It was through their faith that the Lord would warn them to flee or strengthen them in battle according to their need. In response, the "people came running . . . rending their garments . . . as a covenant that they would not forsake the Lord their God."[111]

This then, was a holy army with a righteous cause. Mormon described their leader: "Moroni was a strong and a mighty man; he was a man of perfect understanding; yea, a man that did not delight in bloodshed; a man whose soul did joy in the liberty and the freedom of his country. . . . If all men had been, and were, and ever would be, like unto Moroni, behold, the very powers of hell would have been shaken forever."[112]

Pages 136–37: Beautiful ancient outdoor temple complex at Cambote near Huehuetenango, Guatemala, with the Cuchumatanes in the north. This site has striking similarities to the city of Cumeni in the Book of Mormon. Moroni prepared his people with "all manner of weapons of war."[113] A cimeter was probably a sword-like weapon with pieces of razor-sharp, black obsidian imbedded in it, that could cut a man in half with one stroke.[114]

Above: Stone carving of ancient Mayan warrior at Guatemala City depicting jaguar headdress as a symbol of power. Chief captain Moroni often stopped the battle as the Nephites were winning. He was a man who "did not delight in bloodshed."[115] Amalickiah, on the other hand, swore with an oath to drink Moroni's blood.[116]

Right: The Comitan River valley in southern Mexico is one of the ancient travel corridors to the Pacific and, according to some scholars, may have been where Helaman and his 2,000 stripling warriors marched on their way to take the city of Antiparah.[117]

The war dragged on for at least twelve years because the Nephites' strength was diluted with internal dissension. Those who advocated liberty and followed Moroni were the freemen, but the kingmen were a large group of aristocrats who considered themselves of high birth and wanted power and authority for themselves. They saw the war as an opportunity to topple the reign of judges and establish one of their own with a king. Refusing to defend their country, they wasted their energies in vain aspiration and vying for position.

Thus, in the early years of the war, the Lamanites captured several key Nephite cities near the eastern shore, including Moroni, Nephihah, Lehi, Morianton, Omner, Gid, and Mulek. Meanwhile, several cities on the west sea had also been lost. Absorbed in the eastern battles, Moroni could not come to help Antipus fighting in the west. When, however, the people of Ammon saw the afflictions of the Nephites, they "were moved with compassion . . . to take up arms in the defence of their country."[118] Helaman, however, knowing of their covenant to forever bury their arms, "feared lest by so doing they should lose their souls"[119] and would not allow them this sacrifice. Instead, then, they sent two thousand of their young men, who had not made the holy covenant, to help the desperate Antipus.

Helaman, their leader, wrote of these stripling warriors with tenderness, always calling them "my little sons,"[120] "my little army . . . for they were all of them very young,"[121] but also, he wrote, "never had I seen so great courage."[122] Antipus devised a stratagem whereby this little band would march to Antiparah, where the strongest, most numerous army of the Lamanites were camped, and draw them out of the city. Then, the intent was for the army of Antipus to attack the Lamanites from the rear. Three days and two nights the fierce, innumerable Lamanite army chased the stripling warriors, but on the morning of the third day, they were gone, apparently having turned to attack Antipus. For the moment, at least, the youths were safe.

Helaman asked, "What say ye, my sons, will ye go against them to battle? . . . They never had fought, yet they did not fear death; and they did think more upon the liberty of their fathers than they did upon their lives; yea, they had been taught by their mothers, that if they did not doubt, God would deliver them."[123]

Small streams gather in the highlands and within a few short miles become larger rivers like these near Coban, Guatemala. The Book of Mormon leaves no question that the headwaters of the river Sidon were located in the land of Manti. Many of the armies went to the "head" of the river Sidon to ford it, as the river was a formidable barrier in its lower reaches. By 73 B.C., travel in the Book of Mormon took place along established paths that were often used. Trade had greatly expanded, and no longer did wanderers get lost away from home. The basic course, for example, from Nephi to Zarahemla "eventually became the most important overland route of southern Mesoamerica. This system of trails was the Nephi-Manti-Gideon-Zarahemla route utilized throughout the history of the Book of Mormon as the primary travel corridor between the lands of Zarahemla . . . and the southern lands of Nephi."[124]

The stripling warriors returned to fight the terrible Lamanite army. Antipus and his warriors had overtaken them from the rear, but weary from the speed of their long march, they were losing badly when Helaman's little sons arrived. Together the two Nephite groups surrounded the Lamanites and "did slay them; yea, insomuch that they were compelled to deliver up their weapons of war."[125] Helaman began to number his young men, fearing lest there were many of them slain. "But behold," he said, "to my great joy, there had not one soul of them fallen to the earth; yea, and they had fought as if with the strength of God."[126] The stripling warriors had turned the tide for the Nephites.

The Lord's hand was manifested as one by one the Nephites recaptured their strategic cities again without a single death among the stripling warriors. Helaman said, "We do justly ascribe it to the miraculous power of God, because of their exceeding faith . . . that there was a just God, and whosoever did not doubt, that they should be preserved by his marvelous power."[127]

Meanwhile, the armies in both the east and the west were in dangerous tribulation for want of supplies and food. Moroni wrote to Pahoran, the chief judge in Zarahemla, complaining that the armies had "suffered exceedingly great sufferings; yea, even hunger, thirst, and fatigue."[128] But this is not all, he said: "Great has been the slaughter among our people."[129] Where, he wondered, were their supplies? "Can you think to sit upon your thrones in a state of thoughtless stupor?"[130]

Moroni pleaded with an earnestness for his people; Pahoran answered with a noteworthy largesse of spirit, for he took no offense at having been called a neglectful traitor: "I am not angry, but do rejoice in the greatness of your heart."[131]

Pahoran explained that the kingmen had expelled him and taken over the government in Zarahemla. He had been helpless to send aid. "Gather together whatsoever force ye can upon your march hither," he replied, "and we will go speedily against those dissenters, in the strength of our God according to the faith which is in us."[132] Together Pahoran, Moroni, and the freemen of the Nephites recaptured Zarahemla and soon ended the war, always knowing who was behind the victory.

Large trenches like these are only a part of a much larger ancient defensive complex located just outside of Coban, Guatemala, that match the Book of Mormon's description of the stronghold of Manti. Moroni "caused that they should commence laboring in digging a ditch round about the land. . . . And he caused that they should build a breastwork of timbers upon the inner bank of the ditch; and they cast up dirt out of the ditch against the breastwork of timbers."[133] Trees generally grow only on one side of these trenches today, perhaps because of the decomposition of all the timbers from ancient times, providing deposits of organic material for their growth.

Above: Jaguar in the Peten Jungle near Flores, Guatemala. The jaguar was a dual symbol among the ancients, tied to celestial powers on the one side, and to darkness and secret societies on the other. Some people of secret societies "carried on their persons pieces of jaguar skin, of the forehead and chest, and the tip of the tail, the claws, the canines, and the lips to make them powerful, brave and fearsome."[134]

Right: Beautiful morning in valley just south of Coban, Guatemala. Secret combinations led to the demise of the whole Nephite nation. It is no different today. "I testify that wickedness is rapidly expanding in every segment of our society," said President Ezra Taft Benson. "It is more highly organized, more cleverly disguised, and more powerfully promoted than ever before. Secret combinations lusting for power, gain, and glory are flourishing. A secret combination that seeks to overthrow the freedom of all lands, nations, and countries is increasing its evil influence and control over America and the entire world."[135]

When Helaman, the son of Helaman, assumed the chief judgeship in 50 B.C., it was a hot seat. Within about the preceding two years, one chief judge had been murdered at the hands of a secret combination and another slain in war. As is the case with any class-conscious and covetous society for whom wealth and power are the focus, Zarahemla was rife with internal tensions and intrigue.

Societal self-destruction is the natural offshoot of a people whose heart is set upon riches. Thus, an assassin name Kishkumen, representing the band of Gadianton, stole out by night, intending to murder Helaman. Gadianton's band was a secret combination who had entered into a covenant with secret signs and oaths to protect one another so that "they should not suffer for their murders, and their plunderings, and their stealings."[136] Their aim was to murder and rob to get gain. Hidden from society's view, they could use any rotten means to rise to positions of prominence. When position, status, and influence instead of morality become the measure of a society, such secret combinations flourish.

Helaman's servant, however, in disguise had learned of their assassination plans. He met Kishkumen by night, gave him one of the society's secret signs, and then started toward the judgment seat. On the way, Helaman's servant stabbed Kishkumen "even to the heart, that he fell dead without a groan."[137] Though Helaman planned to execute this band of robbers according to the law, they took their flight out of the land by a secret way. Mormon ends this story on an ominous note, "In the end of this book ye shall see that this Gadianton did prove the overthrow, yea, almost the entire destruction of the people of Nephi."[138]

The implication goes further. Zarahemla's corruption would mirror future societies' corruptions and misplaced values. "And whatsoever nation shall uphold such secret combinations, to get power and gain, until they shall spread over the nation, behold, they shall be destroyed. . . . Wherefore, the Lord commandeth you, when ye shall see these things come among you that ye shall awake to a sense of your awful situation."[139]

By the time Helaman's son Nephi took over the judgment seat in 39 B.C., the people of the church were lifted up in the pride of their hearts, oppressing the poor and "making a mock of that which was sacred."[140] Instead of being fortified by the Lord when the Lamanites attacked, because they had boasted in their own strength, "they were left in their own strength"[141] and lost miserably. It was time for a spiritual resurgence. Like Alma before him, Nephi gave up the judgment seat to preach to the people. He knew that "that . . . government . . . which serves not God, and gives no heed to the principles of truth and religion, will be utterly wasted away and destroyed."[142] No law or social program can stop a nation from dissolving when its people have lost their moral fiber.

With his brother Lehi, Nephi went from one city to the next among the Nephites and finally came among the Lamanites, where the two were thrown in prison. They went without food for several days. Then, in their weakened and exhausted condition, their jailers came to slay them. Suddenly Nephi and Lehi were "encircled about as if by fire . . . and when they saw . . . that it burned them not, their hearts did take courage."[143] Then a cloud of darkness overshadowed the other prisoners and "an awful solemn fear came upon them."[144] Out of the cloud came a voice, saying, "Repent ye, repent ye, and seek no more to destroy my servants whom I have sent unto you to declare good tidings. . . . It was not a voice of thunder, neither . . . of a great tumultuous noise, but behold, it was a still voice of perfect mildness, as if it had been a whisper, and it did pierce even to the very soul."[145]

One of the prisoners, a Nephite by birth, turned and saw through the cloud of darkness the faces of Nephi and Lehi, shining as the faces of angels, and "they did lift their eyes to heaven . . . as if talking . . . to some being whom they beheld."[146] The Nephite turned back and beseeched the other prisoners to repent and cry unto the voice. They all began to cry until the cloud of darkness dispersed, every one of them was encircled in the midst of a flaming fire, and they "were filled with that joy which is unspeakable and full of glory."[147]

About three hundred souls at the prison saw and heard these things and, doubting nothing, "were bidden to go forth"[148] to declare them throughout the land. The evidences were so great that most of the Lamanites were converted and became a righteous people. In fact, "their righteousness did exceed that of the Nephites."[149] At last, after five hundred years of fighting, the Lamanite problem was at least temporarily solved. It hadn't been a contest between the good guys and the bad guys after all, for in this life it is hard to distinguish who is who. The fierce Lamanites turned out to be the most steadfast converts; the righteous Nephites lost their way, blinded by the beauty of their own image. Since none is good but God, the only thing mortals can be very good at is repenting. "The righteous are whoever are repenting, and the wicked whoever are not repenting."[150]

For a time, the Nephites and the Lamanites traveled freely in each other's lands, and trade and industry boomed with their resources not dissipated in war. Yet the desire to be lifted up one above another is a powerful temptation, as if looking down on others is some sort of validation of worth. When climbing to the top is all-important, any means will do. It was an invitation for the Gadianton band to dominate again.

The Lamanites knew just how to take care of them, hunting them out and destroying them. The Nephites embraced them, joined them until they spread over the land and obtained the sole management of the government. These are the characteristics of secret combinations. First, they are inspired by Satan, using ancient oaths and covenants that often resurge mysteriously from one generation to the next. Second, they operate in secret so that they may appear outwardly respectable, their members rising to prominent positions in business and government. Third, their objective is power and gain. Often their target is to take over the ruling of government. Fourth, they use a combination of immorality, money, and violence to achieve their ends. "Once you have been warned . . . that things are being run by such elements, then you know very well that if you aspire to power and gain, influence, status and prestige . . . you can only do it by doing everything their way."[151]

Pages 144–45: First light touches the Pyramid of the Moon at Teotihuacan, near Mexico City. The inner structure was built sometime between 150 B.C. and A.D. 200. Located in the land northward, Teotihuacan may be connected to one of the great Nephite migrations of 55 B.C. when "a large company . . . departed out of the land of Zarahemla into the land which was northward."[152] In that same year Hagoth began to build very large ships, launching them into the west sea (perhaps the Pacific Ocean). The Lord's pattern of scattering the righteous to the nethermost parts of the vineyard can be seen here again.

Left: Pit vipers are a common sight in Central America. Nephi taught his people about the type of Christ Moses used: "As he lifted up the brazen serpent in the wilderness, even so shall he be lifted up who should come. And as many as should look upon that serpent should live."[153]

Above: Light touches a small fern growing out of large stones at the ruins of Quirigua in Guatemala.

Carefully cultured corn growing in the highlands of Guatemala. Corn or maize was a staple in the diet of the Nephites. "Although good soil and growing conditions particularly favored a few areas, most Mesoamerican agricultural was not highly productive. Vast areas are mountainous, frost threatened, or heavily forested."[154] We know from the record that in the land of Nephi they planted their fields "even with all manner of seeds, with seeds of corn, and of wheat, and of barley . . . and with seeds of all manner of fruits. . . ."[155] It may be that when populations increased in the Book of Mormon, competition for resources caused some of the frequent wars.[156]

Seeing the Gadianton robbers in the judgment seats of Zarahemla and the people's hearts set upon riches and the praise of men at any cost, even their own souls, Nephi bowed himself upon a tower in his garden and lamented, pouring out his heart to the Lord. Soon the rabble of Zarahemla gathered to hear him. "Even at this time ye are ripening, because of your murders and your fornication and wickedness, for everlasting destruction,"[157] Nephi warned them. Many who were judges and belonged to the Gadiantons were in the gathered multitude and cried out in fury, "Seize the man." As did the people of Jerusalem, they saw the prophet as a threat to morale, saying, "We are powerful, and our cities great, therefore our enemies can have no power over us."[158]

Nothing is so stinging to the wicked as the truth. We, who can turn a few pages in the record and see Zarahemla's destruction, marvel at such blindness, but it springs from a fundamental misunderstanding held to with pigheaded pride. Man is simply not the measure of all things. Any honest person who spends an entire lifetime learning must finally admit he or she knows almost nothing. Yet here is the Lord who knows all, who can shake the earth with the power of His voice, bid the earth lengthen out the day, or dry up the waters of the great deep—and we will not listen. Why? Because in our willfulness, no matter how great His goodness and mercy toward us, "[we] do not desire that the Lord [our] God, who hath created [us], should rule and reign over [us]."[159] Too many of us want to be mighty, important, a god unto ourselves, instead of tasting the sweetness of knowing the true God.

Nephi gave the crowd a firsthand demonstration of the Lord's specific knowledge. Destruction would come and was now even at their doors. He declared, "Go ye in unto the judgment-seat, and search; and behold, your judge is murdered, and he lieth in his blood; and he hath been murdered by his brother."[160] Five ran to see and found the judge dead exactly as Nephi described. Yet, unwilling to accept evidence for what they did not want to believe—God's existence and power—many of those remaining accused and bound Nephi for the crime, calling him a "pretended prophet."[161] Nephi told them further to go find the judge's brother and ask, "Have ye murdered your brother?"[162]

Early morning in the lowland jungle area of northern Guatemala near Playa Grande and the archaeological site of Nine Hills. Near this site the rapids on the Usumacinta (the Chixoy at this point) impede further travel upriver by ship. This, then, might have been as far as the people of Mulek could have gone. It could be that this is the area of Zarahemla, the great capital city of the Nephites. The site that has been identified here, still covered in jungle growth, is an ancient city as large as eighteen miles across. It is interesting to note that "the Hebrew word translated as 'city' had the fundamental meaning of 'temple center.'"[163] Towers, pyramids, mountains, and temples all had similar meanings to the peoples of antiquity; they were holy places where the people could draw nearer to God. To the ancients, the leading lines would point to the heavens and serve to draw upon the powers of Deity.

Above: Glyph carved on wall at the site of Quirigua, Guatemala. Many of the ancient buildings of Mesoamerica were covered with a paint-like dye, with whole cities being bright vermilion or blue. The greatest commentary ever written on the scriptures is found within the scriptures themselves. Nephi, son of Lehi, for instance, gave insight into the metaphor of trampling: "The very God of Israel do men trample under their feet; I say, trample under their feet but I would speak in other words—they set him at naught, and hearken not to the voice of his counsels."[164]

Then, Nephi said, they would "find blood upon the skirts of his cloak."[165] If they asked where the blood had come from, the murderer would give himself away by trembling and looking pale, "as if death had come upon him."[166] The murderer was found, with every detail as Nephi had described, and the multitude dispersed, leaving Nephi alone and still cast down about his people.

The Lord's voice came to him in comfort, "Blessed art thou, Nephi, for those things which thou hast done; for I have beheld how thou hast with unwearyingness declared the word . . . unto this people . . . and I will make thee mighty . . . even that all things shall be done unto thee according to thy word."[167] Sickened by the spiritual state of his people, Nephi requested the Lord to send a famine into the land "to stir them up in remembrance of the Lord their God."[168] It is ironic that when the Lord blesses and prospers His people, they forget Him and trample the Holy One of Israel under their feet. Only affliction turns their hearts back to Him.[169]

A common sport among all the cultures in Mesoamerica was a game played with a rubber ball on a T-shaped court like this. The captain of the winning team was beheaded as a sacrifice to the gods. Religion played the dominant role in the Mayan (possibly Lamanite) cultures, but it was a brutal religion based on priestcraft.

Enormous salt dome forms this jungle-covered hillside in the lowland area at the site of Nueve Cerros (Nine Hills). Lush forest shelters abundant wildlife, including howler monkeys, jaguars, snakes, and colorful birds. A creek that flows out of the north side of this hill has been used by the Maya for centuries to obtain salt. A city the size of Zarahemla must have been supported by a major industry. Perhaps it was the mining of salt. This place has the only inland salt source in the region. If this is the area of Zarahemla, as assumed by some scholars, it would follow the pattern of the Lord leading His people to an area of salt. Zarahemla would turn away from the Lord and be destroyed by fire at the time of the crucifixion (which indicates that much of the city was built of wood) but be rebuilt again to last at least another 300 years.

The famine turned the majority of both the Lamanites and the Nephites to remember the Lord, but within three years the same old strife was stirred up with dissenters committing "murder and plunder; and then they would retreat back into the mountains, and into the wilderness and secret places . . . receiving daily an addition to their numbers."[170] Within another five years the entire society was again ripe for destruction. Mormon wrote frankly, "And thus we can behold how false, and also the unsteadiness of the hearts of the children of men," for when the Lord "doth prosper his people . . . then is the time that they do harden their hearts."[171]

Onto this scene came Samuel the Lamanite, with words of doom for the respectable folks of Zarahemla. These were the self-righteous, oozing with pride and piety, who could not be told anything, especially by a prophet. "If our days had been in the days of our fathers of old," they boasted, "we would not have slain the prophets; we would not have stoned them, and cast them out."[172]

Yet they could not bear Samuel's words, "Ye do always remember your riches."[173] Because their hearts were set foremost on the economy, they would live and die by the economy with every man for himself. What always follows in a deadly pattern is malice, deceit, persecution, and greed. This is the formula for the self-destruction of a nation. With this mentality, Samuel warned, their riches would become slippery, "that whoso shall hide up treasures in the earth shall find them again no more."[174]

What's worse, blinded by their lust for gold, they would not feel the joy of the single most significant event their forefathers had anticipated for generations—the birth of Jesus Christ. "I give unto you a sign," Samuel said, "for five years more cometh, and behold, then cometh the Son of God. . . . Therefore, there shall be one day and a night and a day, as if it were one day and there were no night . . . ye shall know of the rising of the sun and also of its setting . . . nevertheless the night shall not be darkened; and it shall be the night before he is born."[175] A new star would arise, and "there shall be many signs and wonders in heaven . . . insomuch that ye shall fall to the earth."[176] As Samuel preached from Zarahemla's wall, many cast stones or shot arrows at him, some undoubtedly the very people who claimed they would not have stoned the prophets.

Baby coatimundi (cat of the jungle) looks on curiously in trees of southern Mexico. Near Eastern peoples would not have been familiar with this creature as they arrived in this new land.[177] Curiously, as Joseph Smith translated the record of Ether, he left the animal names of cureloms and cumoms,[178] perhaps because there was no English equivalent to what he saw. The same can be said of the crops of neas and sheum.[179]

Pages 154–55: Clouds catch first light as morning moves upon beautiful Lake Atitlan in Guatemala. Rimmed by three major volcanoes, with San Pedro visible at the left, the nine-mile-long by four-mile-wide lake itself is a caldera (a collapsed volcano) over 1,000 feet deep. From the internal clues of the Book of Mormon, this is a likely candidate for the area of the great city of Jerusalem. Wicked Jerusalem was destroyed at the crucifixion, being covered by water. Remnants of an ancient city have been discovered in the depths of this lake.

4 ARISE AND COME FORTH UNTO ME

Nearly five years had passed since Samuel's astounding prophecy, and the time of the Lord's birth drew near. The skeptics who took the "scientific" point of view contended among themselves, saying, "It is not reasonable that such a being as a Christ shall come."[1]

"Not reasonable." "Foolish." "Ignorant." These are the epithets always thrown at the faithful by the "superior" people who will admit only their limited experience as a gauge of truth. To them, the prophecies of Christ were "a wicked tradition . . . handed down to us by our fathers, to cause us that we should believe in some great and marvelous thing which should come to pass, but not among us, but in a land which is far distant . . . [where] we cannot witness with our own eyes that they are true."[2] What they were looking for, of course, was not evidence but a viewpoint that accommodated and justified their sins and faithless hearts.

They enjoyed mocking the believers, saying, "Behold the time is past, and . . . your joy and your faith concerning this thing hath been vain."[3] As the uproar continued, even the believers "began to be very sorrowful"[4] lest these things not come to pass. At last a day was set aside by the persecutors to gather the believers and, in the name of reason, to murder them "except the sign should come to pass, which had been given by Samuel the prophet."[5]

Anguished, Nephi, son of Nephi and grandson of Helaman, went out alone, bowed himself to the earth, and cried mightily to the Lord all that day. At last the voice of the Lord came to him, saying, "Lift up your head and be of good cheer; for behold, the time is at hand, and on this night shall the sign be given, and on the morrow come I into the world."[6]

That night the sun set but there was no darkness, and "the people began to be astonished."[7] Indeed, "all the people upon the face of the whole earth from the west to the east, both in the land north and in the land south, were so exceedingly astonished that they fell to the earth." And when the sun rose the next morning, "they knew that it was the day that the Lord should be born."[8] A similar sign will accompany the Lord's second coming.[9]

Pages 156–57: Mountains and misty valleys of Chiapas, southern Mexico. Two time-reckoning systems had been used for generations by the Nephites, the first being the number of years since Lehi left Jerusalem (c. 600 B.C.), and the second being the number of years since the beginning of the reign of the judges (92 B.C.). After the birth of Christ, all time was reckoned from that year.[10]

Above: Killer trees like this one in Tikal are abundant in the jungles of Guatemala. A tiny vine slowly crawls up the host tree and wraps little shoots harmlessly around the tree. The vine then draws all the life-giving forces from its host, literally sucking the life out of and killing the unaware donor.

Right: Detail of the amazing killer tree after it has destroyed its host. "And thus we see," Alma said of Korihor, "that the devil will not support his children at the last day, but doth speedily drag them down to hell."[11]

All night it was as bright as midday. The sign of the Lord's birth was unmistakable, and the majority of the people were converted. Yet a scant three years later the people "began to be less and less astonished at a sign or a wonder from heaven." In fact, they "began to disbelieve all which they had heard and seen."[12] How could this be? How could they deny their own senses, negate an experience so overpowering that they had fallen to the earth?

What mental gymnastics could Satan use to make those who had seen such a wonder disbelieve? He whispered to their minds "that it was wrought by men and by the power of the devil, to lead away and deceive the hearts of the people."[13] Clever tactic. He taught the people not to deny the event, just the author of it.

This points up, of course, that signs, however magnificent, do not convert unbelievers in a lasting way. Signs are too easy for the spiritually blind to rationalize away. "It wasn't God," they say. "It was luck. It was a natural circumstance." Time clouds the impact upon us. Signs are not meant for the conversion of the heart. Instead, the Lord told us, "Signs . . . *follow* them that believe."[14] They are the natural result of faith.

It is clear from scripture that even those with a will to believe have short memories. For the children of Israel enslaved by Pharaoh, the Lord turned a river to blood, sent plagues of frogs and flies, sent unnatural hail, fire, and darkness upon Egypt—all to free them. Very impressive stuff. Yet they quickly forgot who led them, crying in the desert, "It had been better for us to serve the Egyptians, than that we should die in the wilderness."[15] Those who cheered Jesus Christ on the Sunday of His triumphal entry into Jerusalem had nothing but silence for Him five days later as He bent under the weight of a cross on His way to Golgotha.

No wonder, then, that memory is a theme of the Book of Mormon. The angel told Alma the younger to "remember the captivity of thy fathers"[16] and Who had spared them. He, in turn, told the people of Ammonihah to remember that Lehi "was brought out of Jerusalem by the hand of God."[17] It is a plea to us, too. The Lord touches us, we know it, and then the weight of the here and now makes us forget. Ancient prophets plead, "Remember."

Soft tones of color such as these tree blossoms fill the jungles along the Dulce River in eastern Guatemala. The gathering of the righteous among the Nephites and the Lamanites to fortify against the Gadianton robbers is a type of the last days when all the righteous must gather to stand against the evils of the world. "And with one heart and with one mind"[18] will the faithful gather, "and it shall be called the New Jerusalem, a land of peace, a city of refuge, a place of safety for the saints of the Most High God; and the glory of the Lord shall be there . . . insomuch that the wicked will not come unto it, and it shall be called Zion."[19]

In A.D. 16, the fierce Gadianton robbers, like a plague, had begun again to waste cities and spread death and carnage throughout the land. Giddianhi, their arrogant, conceited, and brutal leader sent a letter to Lachoneus, the righteous chief judge. It was a model of self-deception. He began with false and oily praise for Lachoneus "in maintaining that which ye suppose to be your right."[20] Then he belittled him "that ye should be so foolish and vain as to suppose that ye can stand against so many brave men who are at my command."[21] He described his own vicious men as having an "unconquerable spirit" and justified their evil plundering as noble "because of the many wrongs which ye have done unto them."[22] Next, Giddianhi painted himself as charitable and the Nephites as misguided, "feeling for your welfare, because of your firmness in that which ye believe to be right."[23] His offer was for the Nephites to yield up all their possessions and join them in their secret works, which, he said, "I know to be good."[24]

Why preserve this letter in such detail in the record? Probably because Mormon knew the book was for us in the latter days when evil would be called good and good evil, when the darkest kind of behavior would be considered enlightened, and moral standards considered dangerously ultraconservative. Relabeling is the name of the game for the wicked, who can excuse anything by calling it good, broad-minded, a right, an expression of freedom.

Because Giddianhi swore to slay the Nephites "until [they] shall become extinct,"[25] the Nephites began to prepare for what would be the most terrible, bloody battle they had ever fought. They prepared not just by arming themselves but also by prayer. Lachoneus told them, "Except ye repent of all your iniquities, and cry unto the Lord, ye will in nowise be delivered out of the hands of those Gadianton robbers."[26]

At first, the people wanted to take the offensive in the war, but the Lord always forbids that of His people unless He so commands. Instead, they gathered their cattle, flocks, herds, grain, and all their substance so that they could subsist for seven years and marched by the tens of thousands to a strategic, fortifiable part of the land ready to defend themselves. The Gadiantons, accustomed to living on plunder, began to starve.

A narrow neck of land runs nearly two hundred miles along the Pacific coast of Guatemala and Mexico and has served as the primary north-south corridor of travel for millennia. It is bordered on the west by the Pacific and on the east by a formidable mountain land barrier—the Sierra Madre mountain range.[27] In the area shown, the neck narrows, and there is a natural pass that leads into the land northward. Heavy fortifications have been discovered at this site just south of Tonala, Mexico.[28] Just to the north of this pass the land is dry and desolate—to the south it is rich and verdant.[29] Because of all the natural defenses here and the archaeological evidences in the area that match the descriptions from the Book of Mormon, some scholars believe this may be the region where the people gathered together to stand firm against the Gadiantons. The references in the Book of Mormon do not give a clear indication that the narrow neck of land is sur- rounded by water, only that there is a sea on the west.[30] The distance across this line between the two ecosystems at the north end of this narrow neck of land is about a day and a half's journey.[31]

Pages 162–63: Dry ecosystem in eastern Guatemala near the city of Zacapa. Amid all the wickedness and tribal division, the voice of the prophet Nephi was raised, "and . . . they were angry with him, even because he had greater power than they . . . for so great was his faith on the Lord Jesus Christ that angels did minister unto him daily."[32]

161

Heads shorn, bodies dyed in blood, their loins girded in lambskins, hungry with blood lust and hate, the warriors of Giddianhi gathered in awful splendor in the sixth month of A.D. 19, and "great and terrible was the appearance of the armies of Giddianhi."[33] Their leader had sworn a blood-oath to decimate the Nephites, and this was an army capable of the job. "Behold, great and terrible was the day that they did come up to battle."[34]

Seeing the army's appearance, the Nephites fell to the earth, pleading with the Lord for deliverance. In the hours and battles that followed, despite the Gadiantons' terrible threatenings and oaths, the Nephites prevailed. Thus, with all their might, the fiercest army could not destroy the Nephite civilization. Yet eleven years later, with no army opposing them, the Nephite social structure utterly collapsed. What happened?

In A.D. 26, the Nephites returned to their own lands and, Mormon tells us, "there was not a living soul among all the people of the Nephites who did doubt in the least the words of all the holy prophets."[35] Yet, home again and prospering, "there became a great inequality in all the land."[36] In the Book of Mormon, without exception, this is always the beginning of woes. The Lord's people are one; the prophets plead for equality. Satan finds ways to divide us with envy, pride, and fear. A little division leads to more. Special interest groups dominate. Everyone is offended. Both the oppressor and the oppressed become filled with enmity. Like a game of king-of-the-mountain, there are no rules but winning.

"And the people began to be distinguished by ranks, according to their riches and their chances for learning."[37] The record, again, hits the mark. In Mesoamerica, the priests and rulers often held power by claiming both birthright and special knowledge.

Prophets came with warning voices and were secretly murdered by the judges or stoned by the people. The chief judge himself was assassinated by those wanting a king. Finally, the people were so divided that their social system crumbled into tribes, doing to themselves what Giddianhi's army couldn't do.

Above: Volcanic activity has affected many areas of Central America, including this ash-fall deposit in the Tuxtla Mountains in the state of Veracruz, Mexico. Many of the flows in the region date to around A.D. 34. Back-country explorations of sites in Mesoamerica reveal human bones and pottery at the eroded base of 30- and 40-foot-thick lava flows.

Right: Evening light touches a massive 17,295-foot volcano, Iztaccihuatl, just southeast of Mexico City. The 17,845-foot Popocatepetl rises just to the south, with 18,851-foot Citlaltepetl being the highest volcano in the region to the east at Orizaba. Scores of volcanoes rim these lands, making the region unstable with frequent earthquakes and eruptions.

The earth responds to humanity's actions. Nature is in intimate relationship with man. It fell when Adam fell. It gave rain in due season and grain in the fields when Israel obeyed the Lord's commands. Thus, it is somehow fitting that the earth responded with violence and impenetrable darkness when its creator, Jesus Christ, was crucified.

Samuel the Lamanite had prophesied that darkness would cover the land for the space of three days, so in A.D. 33 the people began to watch for the sign "with great earnestness."[38] Then, on the fourth day of the first month of the thirty-fourth year, "there arose a great storm, such an one as never had been known in all the land."[39] Up until that moment, most of the people were sure the prophets had been wrong.

The next three hours contained a physical holocaust beyond experience or imagination. Thunder shook the whole earth; "exceedingly sharp lightnings"[40] such as never had been known in all the land filled the skies; whirlwinds and tempests carried people away. Most likely volcanoes erupted, sending lava flows to bury cities. By far the worst, however, was an upheaval and quaking of the earth so that the "whole face of the land was changed."[41] Earthquakes of only a few minutes issue such immense power as to thrust up land masses and devastate cities. Imagine the raw force of one that could have lasted much of three hours. Zarahemla was taken by flames, and fifteen other named cities were destroyed by fire, buried in the earth, or sunk in the waters.

This picture of destruction fits the Mesoamerican scene, where violent earthquakes are common along the edge of the Pacific basin and scores of volcanoes, many still active in recent history, dot the landscape. "A description of the eruption of Conseguina volcano in Nicaragua in 1835 hints at the terror. . . . A dense cloud first rose above the cone, and within a couple of hours it 'enveloped everything in the greatest darkness.' . . . Fear-struck wild animals blundered into settlements. . . . Then came quakes, 'a perpetual undulation.' Volcanic ash began to fall, like 'fine powder-like flour.' . . . Dust thrown up into the atmosphere combined with heat from the volcano to trigger the storms."[42]

Dark clouds block the light of the afternoon sun as a storm builds around Lake Atitlan in Guatemala. In the center of the amazingly accurate Aztec Calendar stone is a central figure representing the Sun god. Four squares surround the center, suggesting four time periods of great destructions that have come and will come upon the earth. One of these is called the "Sun of Earth," representing a time when great destruction occurred because of heavy earthquakes.[43] Apparently, during the three days of darkness, there were numerous aftershocks, for, in the morning, as the darkness began to disperse, "the rocks did cease to rend, and the dreadful groanings did cease."[44] Mormon doesn't miss the opportunity to teach us about the exactness of the Lord's words being fulfilled: "Whoso readeth, let him understand; he that hath the scriptures, let him search them, and see and behold if all these deaths and destructions . . . are not unto the fulfilling of the prophecies of many of the holy prophets."[45]

At the end of the horrifying three hours, a thick darkness gathered upon the land so that the survivors "could feel the vapor of darkness"[46] as if it were so dense it pressed upon them. "And there could be no light, because of the darkness."[47] Neither candles nor torches nor fire could pierce it. Neither the sun nor the moon nor the stars could show any glimmer. The darkness had extinguished the light. It was as if the earth had fallen from the sun, as if the Lord, the true source of the light, had left the world. Only the Egyptians who held Israel hostage had ever experienced and then recorded anything like it.

For three days no light was seen, but "there was great mourning and howling and weeping among all the people continually; yea, great were the groanings of the people, because of the darkness and the great destruction which had come upon them."[48] In one place they cried, "O that we had repented before this great and terrible day, and then would our brethren have been spared, and they would not have been burned in that great city Zarahemla."[49] In another place they were heard to mourn, "O that we had repented before this great and terrible day, and had not killed and stoned the prophets, and cast them out; then would our mothers and our fair daughters, and our children have been spared."[50]

These events are a type of the Second Coming, when the people in self-satisfied abandonment will still be "eating and drinking, marrying and giving in marriage"[51] and not know until the very hour that destruction is coming.

Then out of the darkness came a voice to these broken souls: "Wo, wo, wo unto this people. . . . O all ye that are spared because ye were more righteous than they, will ye not now return unto me, and repent of your sins, and be converted, that I may heal you? . . . Behold, I am Jesus Christ the Son of God."[52]

Where there had been howlings, now there was silence for the space of many hours. Then through the darkness, the voice came again: "O ye people of the house of Israel, who have fallen . . . how oft would I have gathered you as a hen gathereth her chickens, and ye would not. . . . Return unto me with full purpose of heart."[53] When He had finished speaking, the people began "to weep and howl again because of the loss of their kindred and friends."[54]

Three days had passed away, and in the morning the darkness lifted and the earth ceased its dreadful groanings. At last, "all the tumultuous noises did pass away."[55] With the earth silent, flooded with light, those still alive stopped wailing, and "their mourning was turned into joy."[56] The destruction had been selective. Those left were "the more righteous part of the people . . . who received the prophets and stoned them not."[57]

They must have turned to rebuilding their world, for several months apparently passed. Before the end of A.D. 34, twenty-five hundred of them gathered at the temple in the land Bountiful. This was probably not a random gathering but one full of anticipation. Before Nephi crossed to the promised land, he had known that the resurrected Lord would visit his people. We know, too, that for at least a hundred years the general population had been taught this as well, for in 78 B.C. the people had asked Alma where the Son of God should come. Though the record gives us no details, the people probably knew more about when and where the Lord would come than we usually suppose.

As they gathered at the temple, "marveling and wondering one with another,"[58] they talked of the changes that had taken place and of Jesus Christ. While thus conversing, "they heard a voice as if it came out of heaven; and they cast their eyes round about, for they understood not the voice which they heard; and it was not a harsh voice, neither was it a loud voice; nevertheless, and notwithstanding it being a small voice it did pierce them that did hear to the center, insomuch that there was no part of their frame that it did not cause to quake; yea, it did pierce them to the very soul, and did cause their hearts to burn."[59]

Three times they heard the voice before they could understand. It was God the Father saying, "Behold my Beloved Son, in whom I am well pleased . . . hear ye him."[60] As the multitude cast their eyes toward heaven, "they saw a Man descending out of heaven . . . clothed in a white robe; and he came down and stood in the midst of them; and the eyes of the whole multitude were turned upon him, and they durst not open their mouths."[61]

He stretched forth His hand and said, "Behold, I am Jesus Christ, whom the prophets testified shall come into the world."[62]

Left: Bright morning sunlight bursts through trees at Izapa near Tapachula, Mexico. One can learn a great deal here about the plan of salvation, including the nature of death, resurrection, and the knowledge of a pre-mortal existence. When the Lord comes, the Jews will look upon Him and say, "What are these wounds in thine hands and in thy feet?" Then He will say to them, "These wounds are the wounds with which I was wounded in the house of my friends. I am he who was lifted up. I am Jesus that was crucified. I am the Son of God."[63]

Above: Afternoon glow highlights earthquake damage at Mixco Viejo in Guatemala. The voice of the Father was heard by the people at Bountiful. His words are largely obscured and missing in the Bible, but the Book of Mormon records 944 of them, including, "He that endureth to the end, the same shall be saved,"[64] and "Repent ye, and be baptized in the name of my Beloved Son."[65] Most assuring of all, if we do all things we are commanded and endure to the end, "thus saith the Father: Ye shall have eternal life."[66]

169

How does a God minister to His children when He is with them, face to face? Jesus Christ's visit to this people in the Americas gives us the most personal glimpse of any in scripture.

He began with the message of greatest import, His gift, given not to them as an anonymous congregation but to each individual soul, known of Him. "I have drunk out of that bitter cup which the Father hath given me, and have glorified the Father in taking upon me the sins of the world,"[67] He said. This was for you, He was saying to each person. Whatever your weakness or anguish, your sorrow or secret burden, I have taken it upon me. I have felt it, paid for it, sweat drops of blood for it.

At His words, the "whole multitude fell to the earth."[68] The Lord said, "Arise and come forth . . . that ye may thrust your hands into my side, and also that ye may feel the prints of the nails in my hands and in my feet, that ye may know that I am . . . the God of the whole earth, and have been slain for the sins of the world."[69]

Again, note the approach. This is not a faceless multitude to Him. It is not enough merely to greet them as a crowd, keep them at a distance. To Him, the very hairs on their head are numbered. He knows their names, the intimate details of their lives. As He did to the woman at the well in Samaria, He could tell them their personal histories. "My sheep hear my voice," He had said in Israel, "and I know them."[70] "I . . . know my sheep."[71] "Fear not, little children," He would later say, "for you are mine, and I have overcome the world."[72] Therefore, He wanted to see them one by one, minister to them privately, and let them feel His wounds, each soul bearing away the knowledge that those wounds were for him or her.

Therefore, "the multitude went forth, and thrust their hands into his side, and did feel the prints of the nails in his hands and in his feet . . . going forth one by one until they had all gone forth."[73]

When they had all touched Him and had witnessed for themselves that what all the holy prophets had taught them was true, they cried out together, "Hosanna! Blessed be the name of the Most High God!"[74] and they fell down at the feet of Jesus and worshiped Him.

Pages 170–71: Morning light at the peaceful site of Izapa near Tapachula, Mexico. One stone from the original temple complex is visible in center left of this picture. According to Dr. F. Richard Hauck, this mound complex is an exact model of the Temple of Solomon but in grander proportions. Certainly, any archaeologist unfamiliar with the Book of Mormon who noticed this similarity would be left with startling questions.[75] It is not unlikely that this outdoor temple was especially prepared as the place for

the coming of the Lord. It has all the features of the ancient temple, the Holy of Holies, the inner court, the outer court and altars. This site is a likely candidate for the land of Bountiful where the Savior visited His people.

Above: Northwest corner of the Temple of Quetzalcoatl at Teotihuacan shows multiple use of the feathered serpent with the head of a jaguar. Quetzalcoatl and the legends surrounding this "white God" are tied very closely by some Latter-day Saints with the Lord's visit to the

Nephites. From Indian legends and written records, we learn that both Quetzalcoatl and Christ were recognized as creator of all things. Both were born of virgins. Both were white and came wearing a white robe. Both taught the ordinance of baptism. Both are associated with great destruction at the same time in history. Both sent disciples to preach their word. A new star appears with both. The children of Christ and Quetzalcoatl will become lords and heirs of the earth. Both promised they would come again.[76]

172

To the awed multitude, Jesus issued an invitation to "repent, and become as a little child, and be baptized in my name."[77] His teaching to them, very much like the Sermon on the Mount, described a way of life not so dependent on outward performances as on the condition of the heart, that broken heart and contrite spirit from which all else would flow. It was startlingly, radically different from the world's standards of success, a way of being and responding that only the Lord could design. Those of us in the world, in fact, would be tempted to call it unworkable. Where do we see meekness or a thirst for righteousness taught in self-help books or business seminars as a way to get ahead?

Yet, somehow, this is precisely the Lord's point. Those of us who would be with Him in the kingdom can't be too comfortable in the world. Too often when we think we've found our place in the world, it is just that it has found its place in us.

If the world says to look out for number one, the Lord says to look to Him and "ask, and it shall be given unto you."[78] If the world says accumulate wealth at any cost, the Lord said, "if any man . . . take away thy coat, let him have thy cloak also."[79] If the world says to create a good impression and have the glory of men, the Lord says to do "thine alms . . . in secret."[80] If the world teaches us insecurity and nagging worry, the Lord says to "take no thought for your life. . . . Which of you by taking thought can add one cubit unto his stature?"[81]

"Blessed are the meek,"[82] not the mighty, for they are easy to be entreated, teachable, open to the Lord's guidance. It is the first Nephi asking the Lord where to look for food, Alma going "speedily" back to brutal Ammonihah without a whimper.

"Blessed are the merciful,"[83] not the contentious. Only the merciful refuse to pass cutting judgment; they forgive easily, don't take offense. It is Captain Moroni stopping battles to cease bloodshed, Ammon preaching the gospel to his people's most bitter enemies.

If the natural man commits adultery, the Lord asks that we remove the slightest trace of lust from our hearts. If the natural man contends, the Lord asks us to be peacemakers. Though the world wallows in revenge, the Lord even asks us to love our enemies.

Sculpted jaguar head with plumes of a quetzal bird and the body of a serpent like a rattlesnake adorn the Temple of Quetzalcoatl at Teotihuacan north of Mexico City. These Mesoamerican symbols represent the white god, Quetzalcoatl, who legend says visited these people. Indian tribes from the Aleutian Islands to the tip of South America know of Quetzalcoatl. Traditionally, the jaguar head represents power, the feathers symbolize the heavens and the ability to fly, the serpent body connects to the underworld and the creation.

With the Lord's atonement and resurrection, the law of Moses was fulfilled, and therefore these strict observances that the people had followed for six hundred years in the promised land were now to end—a major change in their daily lives for each of them. The Lord wanted them to know, however, that He had always and would always remember His covenant people. Referring to them, He had told His flock at Jerusalem, "Other sheep I have which are not of this fold; them also I must bring, and they shall hear my voice; and there shall be one fold, and one shepherd."[84]

Then, after calling twelve disciples and teaching for hours, Jesus "looked round about again on the multitude" and said, "Behold, my time is at hand. I perceive that ye are weak, that ye cannot understand all my words. . . . Therefore, go ye unto your homes, and ponder upon the things which I have said . . . and prepare your minds for the morrow, and I come unto you again."[85]

When Jesus had finished speaking, "He cast his eyes round about again on the multitude, and beheld they were in tears, and did look steadfastly upon him as if they would ask him to tarry a little longer with them."[86] Here we see His intimate caring, for their longing for Him to be with them was enough to make Him stay.

"Behold," He said, "my bowels are filled with compassion towards you. Have ye any that are sick among you? Bring them hither. Have ye any that are lame, or blind, or halt, or maimed, or leprous, or that are withered, or that are deaf, or that are afflicted in any manner? Bring them hither and I will heal them."[87] Imagine the group that came forward, little children in their parents' arms, the lame leaning against their friends, those that had been maimed in war or in the mighty destruction. What family would not have been affected? The afflicted must have been quite a number, for, in fact, the record says that when He had spoken, "all the multitude, with one accord, did go forth," and He healed the needy.[88]

Then with unspeakable joy both the healed and the whole bowed at His feet, worshipping Him. Finally, as many as could come forward did kiss His feet and bathe them with their tears.

174

Pages 174–75: Late afternoon light pierces the magnificent rain-forest jungle at Misol-ha in Chiapas, Mexico. As the Lord asked the multitude to come forth and be healed, He added a significant phrase: "for I see that your faith is sufficient that I should heal you."[89] Nephi taught that "the Lord is able to do all things according to his will, for the children of men, if it so be that they exercise faith in him."[90] The Lord told the multitude, "So great faith have I never seen among all the Jews; wherefore I could not show unto them so great miracles, because of their unbelief."[91]

Above: Early morning mists surround hills and fill valleys of Chiapas, Mexico, near Ocosingo with a heavenly glow. With great love Jesus taught the children, "and he did loose their tongues, and they did speak unto their fathers great and marvelous things, even greater than he had revealed unto the people . . . and [the multitude] saw and heard these children; yea, even babes did open their mouths and utter marvelous things; and the things which they did utter were forbidden that there should not any man write them."[92]

Next, the Lord asked the people to bring forth their little children and set them round about Him. Then He commanded the multitude that they should kneel upon the ground. As they did so, heads bowed, He offered a prayer to His Father that was so intimate and powerful that the recorder's words failed him. What is barely glimpsed, merely hinted at, is that the bond between two divine beings, the Father and His adoring Son, so far exceeds any love we understand on earth that mortals are simply left awed and speechless before it. What we experience as love in mortality is only the merest shadow of divine love.

"Jesus groaned within himself,"[93] groaned as He did just before He had raised Lazarus, the groaning and yearning of a God. He prayed, "Father, I am troubled because of the wickedness of the people of the house of Israel."[94] Then, kneeling, "He prayed unto the Father, and the things which he prayed cannot be written, and the multitude did bear record who heard him. And after this manner do they bear record: The eye hath never seen, neither hath the ear heard, before, so great and marvelous things as we saw and heard Jesus speak unto the Father; and no tongue can speak, neither can there be written by any man, neither can the hearts of men conceive so great and marvelous things as we both saw and heard Jesus speak; and no one can conceive of the joy which filled our souls at the time we heard him pray for us unto the Father."[95]

We who are sometimes tempted to hold part of ourselves back from God, a little part reserved for us, must take note that complete submission marks this relationship of Son to Father. Jesus said, "This is the gospel which I have given unto you—that I came into the world to do the will of my Father, because my Father sent me."[96] All our obedience is incomplete until we are willing to take the last leap of total trust and submission.

His prayer completed, Jesus wept at the faith of the multitude, saying, "Behold, my joy is full."[97] Then "he took their little children, one by one, and blessed them" and prayed for them. And as the multitude looked, "they cast their eyes towards heaven, and they saw the heavens open, and they saw angels descending out of heaven as it were in the midst of fire; . . . and the angels did minister unto them."[98]

The ominous black jaguar still roams the jungles of Mesoamerica. Mayan frescos show these animals in royal courts, perhaps as pets. The multitude of children, the number of whom is not included in the record, would grow up as part of a perfect society that would last nearly 165 years. We have sparse accounts of other societies that became like this one, but both Enoch[99] and Melchizedek[100] and their people created perfect societies.

Pages 178–79: Morning light touches simple Mayan huts and the edge of the Guatemalan jungle between Chisec and Playa Grande. These huts may be similar to the dwelling places of the Nephites and may explain why Nephite cities could be burned to the ground and then be rebuilt quite rapidly. In the course of the Restoration, Joseph Smith was visited by numerous heavenly messengers, including the twelve disciples of the Nephites. Joseph Smith "seemed to be as familiar with these" twelve Nephite disciples, John Taylor said, "as we are with one another."[101]

To the gathered multitude, the presence of Jesus Christ was incomparably sweet. They hoped that He would never leave them. Therefore, when He had them bring forth bread and wine and administered the sacrament to them, the covenant had special meaning: "If ye do always remember me ye shall have my Spirit to be with you."[102] In a very real way, the Lord could continue with them. In fact, in a world where we can't go a handful of hours without food and water, where our physical dependence is ever before us, the Lord said that for each who partook of the sacramental bread and water, "his soul shall never hunger nor thirst, but shall be filled."[103]

As it was time for the Lord to leave, He touched His twelve disciples, one by one, and gave them the Holy Ghost. Then a cloud overshadowed the multitude so they could not see Jesus, and He ascended again into heaven, promising to return the next day. Before it was yet dark, the people began to spread the word that they had seen Him. "And even all the night it was noised abroad concerning Jesus," and "an exceedingly great number, did labor exceedingly all that night, that they might be on the morrow in the place where Jesus should show himself unto the multitude."[104]

The next day so many gathered that they were divided into twelve groups and taught by the disciples "those same words which Jesus had spoken"[105] without variation. Then the disciples were baptized, and as they came up out of the water, "the Holy Ghost did fall upon them"[106] and they were encircled in fire.

Suddenly, again, Jesus stood in their midst. Asking the disciples to kneel and pray, He went a little way from them and bowed Himself and prayed, saying, "And now Father, I pray . . . for all those who shall believe on their words . . . that I may be in them as thou, Father, art in me, that we may be one."[107] Returning to His disciples, Jesus blessed them, "and his countenance did smile upon them, and the light of his countenance did shine upon them, and behold they were as white as the countenance and also the garments of Jesus; and . . . there could be nothing upon earth so white as the whiteness thereof."[108]

The Book of Mormon contains not even a hundredth part of the things Jesus taught the people, for "he did expound all things, even from the beginning until the time that he should come in his glory."[111] Jesus taught them for three days, and "after that he did show himself . . . oft, and did break bread oft, and bless it, and give it unto them."[112] Why, then, don't we have more of His teachings? Mormon explained, "I was about to write them, all which were engraven upon the plates of Nephi, but the Lord forbade it, saying: I will try the faith of my people." Other plates, yet to come forth at their appointed times, will contain the rest of His teachings.[113]

What the record does show is the Lord vividly painting for them that day when "the elements should melt with fervent heat . . . and the heavens and the earth should pass away,"[114] reminding them that all "shall stand before God, to be judged of their works."[115] Yet His emphasis was on the future of the house of Israel, not just a lineage but all of those people who will covenant with Him, having their garments washed clean in His blood.

"I will remember the covenant which I have made with my people; and I have covenanted with them that I would gather them together in mine own due time,"[116] He promised. In the east, Jerusalem would be their inheritance; in the west in America they would build a New Jerusalem, "and the powers of heaven shall be in the midst of this people."[117]

In the last days, the gospel would be presented first to the Gentiles and then to Israel. If the Gentiles believed and obey, they would be saved. If not, "wo be unto the Gentiles," the Lord said. "I will destroy thy chariots, . . . cut off the cities of thy land, and throw down all thy strongholds. . . . Thy graven images I will also cut off . . . and thou shalt no more worship the works of thy hands; and I will pluck up thy groves out of the midst of thee."[118] In other words, the entire social structure of the Gentiles will fold as they are disarmed, collapse economically, and deteriorate politically.

The believers of Israel will experience something entirely different: "No weapon that is formed against thee shall prosper."[119] In fact, "the mountains shall depart and the hills be removed, but my kindness shall not depart from thee,"[120] the Lord promised Israel.

Jesus asked His disciples, "What is it that ye desire of me, after that I am gone to the Father?"[121] The first Nephi had been asked the same thing by the Spirit: "Behold, what desirest thou?"[122] In asking this question of these righteous ones, the Lord was placing supreme value on the inner longings of their hearts. This is not a God who imposes His will upon His children but rather lets them choose, expressing their own individuality and deepest needs. Ultimately, it is the compliment He pays to each of us. For good or ill, we can have what we choose. Perhaps the most important and most difficult question we must come to grips with in this life, then, is, "What do I really want?" Distracted by the many tasks of mortality, too many of us go through life doing neither what we should do nor what we want to do. Yet in answering the question, "What do I really want?" lies our mission and finally the course of our eternity. Even if it pains Him, the Lord respects our answer. For the disciples, as for Nephi, because of their obedience the Lord was prepared to bless them with their desires.

After they had lived their normal life span, nine of them wanted to "speedily come unto thee in thy kingdom."[123] Three, however, sorrowed in their hearts, "for they durst not speak unto him the thing which they desired."[124] Jesus, however, knew their thoughts, for, like His beloved, John, they wanted to linger on the earth and bring souls unto Him until He should come again.

Granting their wish, the Lord said, "Ye shall never endure the pains of death; but when I shall come in my glory ye shall be changed in the twinkling of an eye from mortality to immortality.... Ye shall not have pain while ye shall dwell in the flesh, neither sorrow save it be for the sins of the world . . . and ye shall sit down in the kingdom of my Father."[125]

Suddenly the heavens were opened, and they were caught up and "saw and heard unspeakable things,"[126] for it seemed to them that "they were changed from this body of flesh into an immortal state, that they could behold the things of God."[127] Thereafter the prisons could not hold them, nor could the wicked "dig pits sufficient to hold them."[128] Three times they were cast into a furnace and twice into a den of wild beasts and received no harm.

Left: Beautiful waters flow from the mountain, having come through the limestone, subterranean water system at Lanquin, Guatemala. The Lord is always aware of the desires of His children. He is the gracious giver. His bounteous giving includes all the gifts of the Spirit: wisdom, knowledge, faith, healing, working mighty miracles, prophecy, and tongues. Grandest of all, though, is that which He reserves for the most faithful, even "eternal life, which gift is the greatest of all the gifts of God."[129]

Above: Egrets are prolific along the beautiful fishing waters of the Dulce River in eastern Guatemala. At the time of the visitations of Christ, disputations had arisen among the people of Nephi concerning the name of the Lord's church. The Lord answered with clarion words, "How be it my church save it be called in my name? For if a church be called in Moses' name then it be Moses' church; or if it be called in the name of a man then it be the church of a man; but if it be called in my name then it is my church, if it so be that they are built upon my gospel."[130]

After Christ's loving visits, by A.D. 36, both the Lamanites and Nephites on all the face of the land were converted. They built a society, like the city of Enoch, based on principles of Zion, where "the love of God . . . did dwell in the hearts of the people."[131] Contentions disappeared; envyings, strifes, tumults, whoredoms and lyings melted away; and "there could not be a happier people among all the people who had been created by the hand of God."[132] The secret was in being of one heart, having "all things common among them; therefore there were not rich and poor, bond and free, but they were all made free, and partakers of the heavenly gift."[133] With these hints, as readers of the Book of Mormon, we yearn to know more about this Zion, which lasted until the year A.D. 201. Yet in a book where every event and sermon was given for a specific purpose, we have a mere twenty-three verses on this perfect society. What does this significant silence mean? Perhaps understanding Zion is a gift we have to earn.

Left: Early morning light touches seed pods deposited by the wind on ancient steps of a building at Chiapa de Corzo, Mexico. The classless society in the era of A.D. 36 to 201 was markedly different from any other time in the history of the Nephites. "There were no robbers, nor murderers, neither were there Lamanites, nor any manner of -ites; but they were in one, the children of Christ, and heirs to the kingdom of God."[134]

Above: Golden light touches one of the restored buildings of Chiapa de Corzo, which was anciently one of the largest cities in the Chiapas depression of Mexico. Around the time of the crucifixion, important buildings in this city burned. "Immediately afterward a drastically different, more restrained cultural development appeared on the scene"[135] with very little archaeological data revealed in the next 150 years. Instead of elaborate, class-conscious burials in this place, for example, common burials were the rule for nearly two centuries.

Losing all sense of their connection to God, people in all ages who turn from Him become class-conscious, divided, and build up churches to get gain. As this seventh century A.D. stone carving in Guatemala City represents, the wearing of costly apparel is a sure sign of apostasy. One of the saddest notes in the Book of Mormon is that after the perfect society of 165 years begins to break down because of pride, "from that time forth they did have their goods and their substance no more common among them."[136] The three Nephites who elected to stay on the earth until the Lord should come again were protected from the harms of the world. The people "did cast them into furnaces of fire, and they came forth receiving no harm. And they also cast them into dens of wild beasts, and they did play with the wild beasts even as a child with a lamb.[137]

I
f 4 Nephi is fairly quiet in its description of a righteous society, it is because it's a primer for our time. We have need to understand the *wicked* society, taking our blinders off just long enough to see where we fit, why we so often have the sense that things are running down. Certainly the recorders give us enough examples of both righteous and wicked societies that their guiding principles are plain.

Thus, in one of the tragic moments of the Book of Mormon, in A.D. 201, the people turn from their happy society into something that seems to them more appealing. The second generation from the coming of the Lord has all but passed away, and by now, having seen it so many times before in the record, we should certainly understand what will happen next. What could possibly have more allure than the goodness they had known? To his people Alma summed it up this way, "Will ye persist in supposing that ye are better one than another?"[138] The question still applies. Satan fell because he wanted to be first, above the rest of us, above God Himself. He uses the same tactic to inspire his followers. All who feel the need to be better than their fellows, to be always right, to grab power, authority, and popularity can be sure of the source of their inspiration.

It is not wealth but its unequal distribution that brings a host of sins. The climbing for it leads us far afield from the truth, which is, "Are we not all beggars? Do we not all depend on the same Being, even God, for all the substance which we have?"[139]

In A.D. 201, it is no surprise, then, that the people began "to be divided into classes"[140] and "lifted up in pride, such as the wearing of costly apparel . . . and of the fine things of the world."[141] They began to create their own churches and despise the power and authority of the disciples of Christ as a reproach to themselves. Where there had been one heart, now they became divided again into Nephites, Lamanites, Josephites, Zoramites, and more. Where there had been joy, there was willful rebellion.

By A.D. 300, the Gadiantons had again spread over the entire land, and "there were none that were righteous save it were the disciples of Jesus."[142]

The Temple of Inscriptions (c. A.D. 600 to 700) is one of only 34 buildings that have been thoroughly excavated from the original 500 identified in the city of Palenque, Mexico. In its heyday all the buildings of the ancient city were painted a bright vermilion. Grandiose and ostentatious buildings are typical of the Mesoamerican world. This temple, like so many of its day, had very little spiritual purpose and was dedicated to honoring one man, the great king Pacal (A.D. 603

to 684). The people who lived here may have been the war-hardened, apostate Lamanites. The city flourished for about 200 years (A.D. 600 to 800). Most of the remains that have been discovered in Mesoamerica do not represent the people of the Lord but rather apostasy and the worship of man-made gods.

Pages 188–89: Morning sun sends streams of light through low-lying, misty valleys in the Tuxtla Mountains of Mexico. From the number of early

fortifications that fill this naturally protected basin, it is clear that large-scale, ancient battles took place here. It could very well be the site of the last battles of the Jaredites and the Nephites. Artifacts in this small basin date to two time periods: 300 to 400 B.C. and A.D. 300 to 400. Archaeologically it appears that large groups came here, not building extensive dwellings but only fortifications, then mysteriously disappeared, leaving huge amounts of artifacts behind.

5 O YE FAIR ONES, HOW IS IT THAT YE COULD HAVE FALLEN!

Mormon, born about A.D. 310, grew up in a dark, chaotic world where miracles had ceased and instead sorceries, witchcrafts, and magic with their attendant rituals obsessed the people. Gadiantons infested the land, which itself was cursed until everyone's treasures became slippery. The Nephites mourned because "no man could keep that which was his own,"[1] yet still they clung obstinately to their ways. Mormon lamented, "A continual scene of wickedness and abominations has been before mine eyes ever since I have been sufficient to behold the ways of man."[2]

Yet Mormon was a bright exception to the rule. At ten years of age he was approached by Ammaron, the keeper of the records, who said, "I perceive that thou art a sober child, and art quick to observe."[3] Therefore he asked that when Mormon was twenty-four years old, he go to the hill Shim where Ammaron had deposited the sacred records, take charge of them, and continue engraving on the plates of Nephi the things that he observed about the people. By the age of fifteen, Mormon had been visited by the Lord and "tasted and knew of the goodness of Jesus."[4]

Left: Ceiba tree stands over 100 feet tall as a lone sentinel on a more than 2,000-foot-long, man-made ridge of dirt in a protected basin in the Tuxtla Mountains of Mexico. Mormon's life has fascinating correlations to that of Joseph Smith. Mormon was eleven when his father "carried him" into the land southward.[5] Joseph Smith was nearly eleven and still crippled from his leg operation when he was carried on a wagon (at times) from New England southward to New York State. Mormon saw the Lord when he was fifteen.[6] Joseph was in his fifteenth year when he had his First Vision. Mormon was about twenty-four when he obtained the plates and began his abridgment. Joseph was about twenty-four when he translated the plates. Mormon was named after his father, as was Joseph.

Above: Spider web catches dew and morning light in the Tuxtla Mountains of Mexico. Some archaeologists believe there are more than 100,000 ancient sites in Mesoamerica. Only a few of these sites have been uncovered or explored.[7]

In his sixteenth year, Mormon became commander of the Nephite army, leading them against the Lamanites. The war would continue for the next fifty-nine years, from A.D. 326 to A.D. 385, with only occasional interludes of calm. With losses at the cities or lands of Angola, David, Joshua, Jashon, and Shem, the Nephites gathered in their people as they fought, then fled west and north out of their homeland, their cities burning around them. As the war dragged on, the brutal Lamanites took the captured women and children and offered them, screaming, as sacrifices to their idol gods. The Lord does not need to punish the wicked; the wicked do it to themselves and to each other.

Such a continual scene of blood sickened Mormon. The Nephites mourned, too, but not unto repentance. It was instead "the sorrowing of the damned, because the Lord would not always suffer them to take happiness in sin."[8] Reduced to a nightmare of carnage and insecurity, they continued to walk "straight to their certain destruction because they were helpless to conceive of acting in any other way. . . . They were so hypnotized by the necessity of what they were doing that they didn't even let the fear of death deter them. . . . This is what the Greeks called *ate*, the point of no return beyond which it becomes impossible to change, and only one solution to a problem remains possible. You simply have to play out the play to the end the way you've been doing it."[9]

"I saw that the day of grace was passed with them, both temporally and spiritually,"[10] said Mormon. Still, filled with the love of God, even for these wicked countrymen, he poured out his soul to God "all the day long for them; nevertheless, it was without faith, because of the hardness of their hearts."[11] In Mormon we see under the most grueling circumstances the meaning of Christ-like love. Instead of abandoning the hysterical and wicked Nephites who had lost their love even for one another, he wrote to his son, "Notwithstanding their hardness, let us labor diligently; for if we should cease to labor, we should be brought under condemnation; for we have a labor to perform whilst in this tabernacle of clay."[12]

Pages 192–93: Spectacular sunset in the area of Arriaga, Mexico, near the Pacific coast. This region fits the description in the Book of Mormon of the land and city of Desolation. At Desolation Mormon utterly refused to be commanding general after 36 years of holding that position.

Above: Eyipantla waterfalls near San Andreas Tuxtla may be part of the "land of many waters, rivers, and fountains"[13] where Mormon had all the Nephites gather for the "last struggle" with the Lamanites. Mormon states that "here we had hope to gain advantage over the Lamanites."[14] It was the same place the Jaredites had come for their last, great battle, likely for the same reason. There were Jaredite fortifications already in place that could be rebuilt. What does Mormon's statement mean? Possible explanations are that, according to legend, this area was associated with ritualistic and spiritual power. It may have also been considered an entrance into the under-world. Here the natural terrain could be used to form a strong, defensive stance.

As long as the Nephites fought a defensive war, Mormon led their armies. But when in the city Desolation they began to boast in their own strength and swore to avenge their brothers' blood in an offensive war, the great general "utterly refused" to continue. He sat out for thirteen years, watching the atrocities in horror. Finally, however, as the Lamanites sought to annihilate his people and expunge their memory from the face of the earth, Mormon took command again, certain that their cause was hope-less, for the people "did struggle for their lives without calling upon that Being who created them."[15]

He refused to describe the holocaust in the record, fearing to offend the reader, but his few references are horrible with both sides guilty of abominations. The Lamanites fed the women and children the flesh of their husbands and fathers. The Nephites raped the Lamanite women and then "devour[ed] their flesh like unto wild beasts"[16] as a token of bravery. All the primitive sav-agery of later Mesoamerican war and apostasy is evident in these lines. What's even more clear, however, is what a world is like when all the light is taken away. No matter how enticing are Satan's initial offers, this is what he finally brings. It is death, both physical and spiritual, a world so black that death is welcome. Satan makes it seem inevitable that the course must simply be pur-sued to its end.

At last, Mormon wrote the king of the Lamanites and asked that the Nephites be allowed to gather their people to the land of Cumorah for a final stand. Cumorah was a good choice defen-sively, but it also may have had some ritual or mythological pull to it. Here the Jaredites had made their final stand, and here they had been completely decimated. Now a second people was about to re-play that same destiny.

For four years the people gathered to Cumorah and built forti-fications for the battle ahead. These were a war-hardened, unruly people, thirsty for blood and hateful to each other. Mormon said, of them, "They were once a delightsome people, and they had Christ for their shepherd; yea, they were led even by God the Father. But now, behold, they are led about by Satan, even as chaff is driven before the wind."[17]

Above: Lower battle complex in a basin area of the Tuxtla Mountains of southern Mexico. Line after line of artificial, defensive mounds, hills, and ridges have been discovered in this area, with artifacts dating to the times of the last battles of the Jaredites and the Nephites.

Left: Defensive and ceremonial complex in the lower battle area of this protected basin in the Tuxtla Mountains of Mexico. If this was the place of the final battle, the Lamanites would have come from the south, which horizon is seen in the right of this picture. For a site to qualify as the last battle area, it must have massive fortifications. The Nephites did not sit down at Cumorah and wait for four years for the appointed day of the battle. Out of love for his people, Mormon would surely have caused fortifications to be erected, as he had in all previous strongholds, with large heaps of earth to be thrown up, and strategies planned to defend themselves against the onslaught of the Lamanites. Sixteen centuries would not have completely hidden these fortifications.

195

The day of the battle arrived, "and it came to pass that my people, with their wives and their children, did now behold the armies of the Lamanites marching towards them; and with that awful fear of death which fills the breasts of all the wicked, did they await to receive them."[18] The Nephite army was 230,000 strong plus their women and children who may have been armed, if only for self-defense. But the Lamanite army that fell upon them was innumerable. "Every soul was filled with terror because of the greatness of their numbers."[19]

With the women clutching their children, looking desperately for someplace to hide, the vulnerable were massacred with the rest. Four years of effort in fortifications were trampled in short order by an army bent on Nephite decimation. The Lamanites fell mercilessly upon Mormon's people with the sword, the bow, the arrow, and the ax. The screams and howling would have been deafening. There was no place to retreat, nothing for some of the weaker or younger to do but wait for death.

It was over in a single day.[20] Mormon's ten thousand were all hewn down. Because he fell wounded amid the bodies, the Lamanites passed by him and did not kill him. The next day, when the Lamanites had returned to their camps, the stricken Mormon made his way to the top of the hill Cumorah, where he found only twenty-three other survivors, including his own son, Moroni.

From that vantage he could see it all, how wave upon wave of Lamanites had slaughtered his entire nation: "Lamah had fallen with his ten thousand; and Gilgal had fallen with his ten thousand; and Limhah had fallen with his ten thousand."[21] On the grim catalog went, the news never getting better. Such an end to his posterity had been seen by a brokenhearted Nephi. Now the prophecy about those who rejected Jesus Christ in this promised land was sadly fulfilled.

As Mormon scanned the possibly more than a million dead before him, he cried, "O ye fair ones, how could ye have departed from the ways of the Lord! O ye fair ones, how could ye have rejected that Jesus, who stood with open arms to receive you!"[22] The Nephite civilization was only a memory on the wind.

Pages 196–97: View from the top of a strategic hill at the north end of this basin in the Tuxtla Mountains. The fog in the middle of the picture outlines a man-made ridge that rims this hill, averaging 30 to 40 feet high and running over 2,000 feet long. On the right is a giant sinkhole that measures about 500 feet across and 200 feet deep with only one natural entry. This could have been used to protect the women and children of the Nephites. The number of women and children who were killed, with the soldiers, could have easily brought the total Nephite dead to over one million. Given a defensive position like this, it is clear that the Lamanites massively outnumbered the Nephites, so the dead Lamanites likely numbered in the millions.

Above: Morning light touches a strategic hill in the north center of the basin complex of the Tuxtla Mountains. From atop this hill, part of which is man-made, the two mile by two and one-half mile basin can easily be seen. Mormon might not have wanted to retreat any farther north from here because of the mighty Teotihuancani people who were militarily the most powerful group in Mesoamerica. Mormon speaks remorsefully "that there were sorceries, and witchcrafts, and magics; and the power of the evil one was wrought upon all the face of the land."[23] This area still attracts these evils and is a world center for witchcraft.

Yet, the Nephites and their message of triumph and tragedy was not to be forgotten. Before the last battle, as his people were gathering to Cumorah, Mormon wrote, "I, Mormon, began to be old; and knowing it to be the last struggle of my people . . . therefore I made this record out of the plates of Nephi, and hid up in the hill Cumorah all the records which had been entrusted to me by the hand of the Lord."[24] The record he prepared is an abridgment of all the Nephite records. Though Mormon couldn't include a hundredth part of his people's doings, what he chose to include was directed by the Lord for a specific purpose—to come forth in a latter-day to a people who, when reading it, would see themselves. It would be directed to the house of Israel, particularly the Lamanites, and to the ends of the earth unto the convincing them that Jesus is the Christ. In its pages, a people living a millennium and a half beyond the last battle would hear the prophets whisper, "Oh, see us and do better."

After the last battle, Mormon's son, Moroni, now the protector of the sacred plates, continued the engraving. "After the great and tremendous battle at Cumorah, behold, the Nephites who had escaped into the country southward were hunted by the Lamanites, until they were all destroyed."[25] It was a national tragedy and a personal one: "My father hath been slain in battle, and all my kinsfolk, and I have not friends nor whither to go; and how long the Lord will suffer that I may live I know not."[26]

Moroni would spend the next thirty-six years essentially alone, the tragic hero, haunted by his memories and hounded by the Lamanites who, having tasted blood, wanted more: "For behold, their wars are exceedingly fierce among themselves; and because of their hatred they put to death every Nephite that will not deny the Christ. And I, Moroni, will not deny the Christ; wherefore, I wander whithersoever I can for the safety of mine own life."[27]

Four times on the plates, Moroni bade farewell, certain that he would be killed. His life was tied up in one thing—his sacred stewardship of the plates, that this voice from the dust could someday speak to a future generation.

Poignant reminder of those who were also involved in that great and last battle of the Nephites is this child's whistle found on one of the battlefields in the Tuxtla Mountains. A haunting, beautiful sound can still be made with this instrument. Every man, woman, and child was filled with terror as the massive Lamanite armies marched toward them. Mormon's unending and tender love of his own son Moroni is evident in his letters to him: "I am mindful of you always in my prayers, continually praying unto God the Father in the name of his Holy Child, Jesus, that he, through his infinite goodness and grace, will keep you through the endurance of faith on his name to the end."[28] Touchingly, Mormon refers to Moroni five times in two epistles as "my beloved son."[29]

Olmec figures with skull deformation on display in Mexico City museum. The name Olmec *is a modern name given to the civilization that inhabited the Gulf of Mexico region of southern Mexico from around 2,500 to 400 B.C. Considered by many "the mother culture" of Mesoamerica, the Olmecs are described in detail by early writer Fernando de Alva Ixtlilxochitl (A.D. 1578-1650). He spoke of the first settlers coming from the great tower at the time of the confusion of languages and of their being able to preserve their language. He wrote of their traveling long distances until they came to a good and fertile land.*[30]
Archaeologically, the Olmecs, as they are called, mysteriously disappeared around 400 B.C.

In his hazardous, solitary world, Moroni must have found some companionship in the voluminous records of the Nephite people in his keeping. Among them was a particular treasure, the twenty-four plates of Ether found by Limhi's people and translated by King Mosiah. On these plates was the history of the Jaredites, who had been led away from the Tower of Babel sometime after 3000 B.C. Like the Nephites after them, the Jaredites had been directed by the Lord to the promised land and given the same covenant: "Whoso should possess this land of promise, from that time henceforth and forever, should serve him, the true and only God, or they should be swept off when the fulness of his wrath should come upon them."[31]

Though the plates Moroni received were nearly full, somewhere, somehow, he evidently found more ore, for he began a major work in abridging Ether to add to the Book of Mormon. It would serve as a second witness to the Nephite history, disquieting in its familiarities. The Jaredites, too, had started with a spiritual leader and a vision. The people had been a blessed colony who had escaped the confounding of their language and were led to the promised land. Their prophet, the brother of Jared, had seen the Lord, Jesus Christ, who had ministered to him and illuminated stones with His finger that they might have light on their ocean journey. In the promised land, they went through cycles of righteousness and wickedness, always reminded by prophets to repent. Finally, utterly rejecting the Lord, they fought a suicidal civil war, ending in the annihilation of their nation at the Hill Riplah, the same hill the Nephites called Cumorah.

Their battle wasn't over in a single day or week or month. When the light is extinguished in a soul, here is what's left. Day after day they fought, men, women, and children armed, retiring to their camps at night to rend the air with their howling and lamentation for the slain. Then, drunk with anger, "even as a man who is drunken with wine,"[32] they slept on their swords and, as if mesmerized in the darkness, returned to their ghoulish fighting another day. Their end, as it had been for the Nephites, was utter destruction sometime after 600 B.C.

Twenty-four-ton basalt head discovered at the ancient site of La Venta, Mexico. To date, twenty-three of these giant heads have been found, all from the Olmec period. Though the Jaredite nation was destroyed, Jaredite cultural overlap is starkly evident throughout the Nephite history. The Nephite weights and measures all bear Jaredite names. The first land the Jaredites settled was Moron, which is closely associated with Moroni (meaning "belonging to Moron" or "of Moron"). The behavior of men with Jaredite names is significant. "Morianton sought to lead a great body of people back into the wilderness; Coriantumr was a notorious apostate and subversive; Korihor rebelled against the church . . . Nehor actually succeeded in setting up a rival system of government . . . oppressive taxation, whoredoms, and abominations."[33] And the very name Gadianton, so similar to the Jaredite Morianton and Corianton, connotes darkness and evil of the blackest pitch. The book of Ether, which is Moroni's abridgment of Jaredite records, mentions at least thirty-three generations of this culture, which came to an end in the land the Nephites called Cumorah.

Standing at the edge of a 200-foot sheer drop looking into the large cenote (sink hole) at the protected basin area of the Tuxtla Mountains in Mexico. If this is the area of the last battles of the Jaredites and the Nephites, millions may have been killed here. Perhaps there is not another place like it on earth in so specific an area. Joseph Smith once entered a woods of recent growth and told the brethren, "I felt much depressed in spirit and lonesome, and that there had been a great deal of bloodshed in that place, remarking that whenever a man of God is in a place where many have been killed, he will feel lonesome and unpleasant, and his spirits will sink."[34] Mormon cried about his people, "How is it that ye could have fallen! But behold, ye are gone, and my sorrows cannot bring your return."[35]

Why bother giving us back-to-back histories of two civilizations who rejected the Savior and then turned on themselves in a frenzy of self-destruction? Isn't it just too much? No. The generation for whom the shoe fits must wear it. Mormon and Moroni knew they were creating this record as a warning and witness for a materialistic, secular people far in the future from their day. Moroni wrote, "I speak unto you as if ye were present, and yet ye are not. But behold, Jesus Christ hath shown you unto me, and I know your doing."[36]

The day he had seen is our day. His description is right on the mark. The book shall come forth, he said, in a day when the power of God is denied, when there are secret combinations and works of darkness, when there are "pollutions upon the face of the earth," when there are murders, robbing, lying, deceiving, and whoredoms; and when all manner of abominations are justified because "it mattereth not."[37] It shall come forth in a day when people "walk in the pride of [their] hearts"[38] and love their substance more than they love the poor and needy.

First light touches gnarled and weather-worn tree anchored to the side of a strategic hill in the Tuxtla Mountains of southern Mexico. Its branches reach out almost in symbol of Mormon's lament for the slain of his people. From internal clues in the Book of Mormon and from all that scholarship can teach us, it appears that the great and last battle of the Nephites may have taken place somewhere in these verdant mountains rather than in western New York as tradition has taught us for generations.

Pages 204–5: Early morning glow before sunrise in the lower battlefields of the protected basin area in the Tuxtla Mountains of Mexico. Moroni recorded the words of the prophet Ether, which surely echoed his own: "Whoso believeth in God might with surety hope for a better world, yea, even a place at the right hand of God, which hope cometh of faith, maketh an anchor to the souls of men, which would make them sure and steadfast, always abounding in good works, being led to glorify God."[39] Moroni wandered for thirty-six years with the abridgment record (the gold plates), the Urim and Thummim, and the breastplate, finally depositing them in a hill that would be not far from where young Joseph Smith would live fourteen centuries later.

Not only does the Book of Mormon point out in chilling detail the foibles of fallen humanity, but in its pages it offers great comfort and protection as well. It is an epistle of love to us of the latter days. If we live in a world where many deny the Lord, this book reminds us that "all that is good cometh of God" and that those who seek Him will find Him. As Jesus Christ did for the Nephites at Bountiful, He stands with His arms outstretched in love toward us, for He is "the same yesterday, today, and forever"[40] "Behold, I will show unto you a God of miracles,"[41] Moroni said, and in this record he did. We learn more of Jesus Christ and his atonement in the pages of this book than in any other source in the world.

If we live in a world where faith is considered naive, the refuge of the childish, the Book of Mormon teaches, "It is by faith that miracles are wrought; and it is by faith that angels appear."[42]

If we have felt battered by a world where people are too often harsh, competitive, and unfeeling, the Book of Mormon teaches us that "charity is the pure love of Christ"[43] which "suffereth long, and is kind, and envieth not, and is not puffed up, seeketh not her own, is not easily provoked."[44]

In the book, we simply learn how to live, not just through sermons but through living sermons. A Nephi who didn't murmur in the wilderness, an Alma who knew the most exquisite joy because he repented, the sons of Mosiah who turned their bitterest enemies into friends through the love of Jesus Christ, a Moroni who stuck loyally by his stewardship with the sacred record for thirty-six lonely years before depositing it in the Hill Cumorah in New York. If in this grim world we have forgotten that such beauty of heart and character exists, it is here. Moroni promised, "When ye shall receive these things, I would exhort you that ye would ask God, the Eternal Father, in the name of Christ, if these things are not true; and if ye shall ask with a sincere heart, with real intent, having faith in Christ, he will manifest the truth of it unto you, by the power of the Holy Ghost. And by the power of the Holy Ghost ye may know the truth of all things."[45]

NOTES

PERSONAL NOTES

1. *Times and Seasons*, 3:927.

PROLOGUE

1. As quoted in Ezra Taft Benson, *An Enemy Hath Done This*, p. xi.

2. Franklin D. Richards and James A. Little, *Compendium* (Salt Lake City: Deseret News Press, 1886), p. 289.

3. B. H. Roberts, *New Witnesses for God* (Salt Lake City: Deseret News, 1909), 2:199–200.

4. *Times and Seasons*, 3:927.

5. John L. Sorenson, *An Ancient American Setting for the Book of Mormon* (Salt Lake City and Provo: Deseret Book and F.A.R.M.S., 1985), p. 124.

6. Ibid.

7. Ibid. p. 129.

8. Ibid. p. 131.

9. Mosiah 8:8

10. Ibid.

11. *Journal of Discourses*, 4:105.

12. *History of the Church*, 2:79–80.

SECTION 1:

LET US BE STRONG LIKE UNTO MOSES

1. 1 Nephi 1:6. See also Dean C. Jessee, ed., *The Papers of Joseph Smith* (Salt Lake City: Deseret Book, 1992), 2:69.

2. See Hugh Nibley, *An Approach to the Book of Mormon* (Salt Lake City and Provo, Utah: Deseret Book and F.A.R.M.S., 1988), p. 71.

3. 1 Nephi 2:12.

4. 1 Nephi 2:11.

5. 1 Nephi 2:16.

6. See 1 Nephi 1:2.

7. Hugh Nibley, *Lehi in the Desert/The World of the Jaredites/There Were Jaredites* (Salt Lake City and Provo, Utah: Deseret Book and F.A.R.M.S., 1988), p. 39.

8. Nibley, *Approach to the Book of Mormon.*, p. 124.

9. 1 Nephi 3:13.

10. 1 Nephi 3:29.

11. 1 Nephi 3:31.

12. Nibley, *Approach to the Book of Mormon*, p. 116.

13. 1 Nephi 4:6.

14. 1 Nephi 4:10.

15. 1 Nephi 4:13.

16. 1 Nephi 4:32.

17. Brigham Young stated this on June 17, 1877, as recorded in *Journal of Discourses*, 19:38.

18. *Journal of Discourses*, 23:184.

19. 1 Nephi 5:2.

20. 1 Nephi 5:8.

21. 1 Nephi 5:14.

22. Don Peretz, *The Middle East Today* (New York: Praeger Publishers, 1988), p. 8.

23. *Major British Writers* (New York: Harcourt, Brace and World, 1959), p. 254.

24. See Genesis 37:19.

25. 1 Nephi 8:10.

26. Alma 32:41.

27. 1 Nephi 8:12.

28. 1 Nephi 8:21.

29. 1 Nephi 12:18.

30. 1 Nephi 8:1.

31. 1 Nephi 8:24.

32. 1 Nephi 15:24.

33. 1 Nephi 8:26–27.

34. Lucy Mack Smith, *History of Joseph Smith by His Mother* (Salt Lake City: Bookcraft, 1958), p. 49.

35. Ibid., p. 50.

36. 1 Nephi 10:17.

37. 1 Nephi 10:19.

38. 1 Nephi 11:1 (italics added).

39. Ibid.

40. 1 Nephi 11:11.

41. 1 Nephi 11:2.

42. 1 Nephi 11:3.

43. 1 Nephi 11:15.

44. 1 Nephi 11:21.

45. Ibid.

46. 1 Nephi 2:9.

47. 1 Nephi 15:5.

48. Ether 2:12.

49. See Alma 34:10.

50. 1 Nephi 11:25.

51. 1 Nephi 13:39.

52. Ibid.

53. 1 Nephi 12:18.

54. Smith, *History of Joseph Smith by His Mother*, p. 50.

55. See 1 Nephi 13:12.

56. See 1 Nephi 13:13.

57. See 1 Nephi 13:17–19.

58. 1 Nephi 13:40.

59. See 1 Nephi 14:28.

60. Words of Mormon 1:5.

61. Ether 15:33.

62. Joseph Smith–History 1:41.

63. John 21: 25.

64. 1 Nephi 1:25.

65. Alan K. Parrish, in *The Book of Mormon: First Nephi, The Doctrinal Foundation* (Provo, Utah: Religious Studies Center, Brigham Young University, 1988), pp. 134–35.

66. Ibid., p. 135.

67. Ibid., p. 140.

68. 1 Nephi 15:8.

69. 3 Nephi 14:7.

70. 1 Nephi 15:9.

71. 1 Nephi 9:6.

72. 1 Nephi 9:5.

73. 1 Nephi 11:17.

74. Alma 37:40.

75. 1 Nephi 17:30.

76. 1 Nephi 4:21.

77. Lynn and Hope Hilton, *In Search of Lehi's Trail* (Salt Lake City: Deseret Book, 1976), p. 16.

78. 1 Nephi 16:31.

79. 1 Nephi 17:12.

80. Nibley, *Lehi in the Desert*, p. 64.

81. Ibid.

82. 1 Nephi 16:19.

83. Ibid.

84. 1 Nephi 16:23.

85. Nibley, *Lehi in the Desert*. p. 232.

86. See 1 Nephi 16:34.

87. Warren P. and Michaela J. Aston, "The Place Which Was Called Nahom" (Provo, Utah: F.A.R.M.S., 1991), p. 8.

88. 1 Nephi 16:35.

89. 1 Nephi 16:34.

90. 1 Nephi 16:38.

91. *The Koran*, trans. with notes by N.J. Dawood (London: Penguin Books, 1974), p. 133.

92. See 1 Nephi 19:2.

93. As quoted in Nibley, *Lehi in the Desert*, p. 65.

94. Ibid.

95. Ibid.

96. 1 Nephi 17:31.

97. Alexandre Dumas, *The Count of Monte Cristo* (New York: Bantam Books), p. 34.

98. 2 Nephi 25:23.

99. 1 Nephi 17:13.

100. 2 Nephi 4:19.

101. 1 Nephi 16:32.

102. 1 Nephi 17:2–3.

103. 1 Nephi 17:20–21.

104. 1 Nephi 17:5.

105. 2 Nephi 31:20.

106. 1 Nephi 17:5.

107. See Aston and Aston, "And We Called the Place Bountiful" (Provo, Utah: F.A.R.M.S., 1991).

108. See Jacob 5:13.

109. 1 Nephi 17:5–6.

110. 1 Nephi 17:7.

111. 1 Nephi 17:8.

112. 1 Nephi 17:9.

113. 1 Nephi 17:11.

114. 1 Nephi 17:16.

115. 1 Nephi 17:13–14.

116. 1 Nephi 18:3.

117. 1 Nephi 18:2.

118. See 1 Nephi 17:11.

119. 1 Nephi 17:17.

120. 1 Nephi 17:19.

121. 1 Nephi 17:22.

122. 1 Nephi 17:50–51.

123. 1 Nephi 17:5.

124. 1 Nephi 17:48.

125. 1 Nephi 16:2.

126. 1 Nephi 17:48.

127. 1 Nephi 17:52.

128. 1 Nephi 17:53.

129. 1 Nephi 17:55.

130. 1 Nephi 18:3.

131. 1 Nephi 18:1.

132. Nephi 10:12.

133. Jacob 7:26.

134. 1 Nephi 18:6.

135. 1 Nephi 18:6.

136. 1 Nephi 18:9.

137. 1 Nephi 18:10.

138. 1 Nephi 18:12–13.

139. 1 Nephi 18:13.

140. 1 Nephi 18:17–18.

141. 1 Nephi 18:20.

142. 1 Nephi 18:15.

143. 1 Nephi 18:16.

144. 1 Nephi 18:21.

145. 1 Nephi 18:22.

146. 1 Nephi 18:5.

SECTION 2:

THIS PRECIOUS LAND OF PROMISE

1. 1 Nephi 18:24.

2. 1 Nephi 18:25.

3. 2 Nephi 1:7, 10.

4. Sorenson, *Ancient American Setting*, p. 146.

5. Jacob 7:1, 4.

6. Sorenson, *Ancient American Setting*, p. 74.

7. 2 Nephi 1:14.

8. 2 Nephi 2:11.

9. 2 Nephi 2:23.

10. 2 Nephi 2:27.

11. See JST, Genesis 50:24–37.

12. 2 Nephi 3:4–5.

13. 2 Nephi 3:6.

14. 2 Nephi 3:15.

15. 2 Nephi 3:12.

16. 1 Nephi 14:23.

17. 1 Nephi 13:26, 29.

18. See Explanatory Introduction to the Doctrine and Covenants.

19. See Mosiah 21:25; 22:15–16.

20. See Alma 22:27–29; 50:7–9, 11.

21. 2 Nephi 4:16–34.

22. Jacob 6:5.

23. Nibley, *Approach to the Book of Mormon*, p. 401.

24. 2 Nephi 5:6.

25. 2 Nephi 5:11, 27.

26. 2 Nephi 5:24.

27. Jacob 1:19.

28. Ibid.

29. See 2 Nephi 10:3.

30. 2 Nephi 10:5.

31. Jacob 4:4.

32. 2 Nephi 9:13.

33. 2 Nephi 9:10.

34. 2 Nephi 9:9.

35. 2 Nephi 9:50.

36. 1 Nephi 20:1. See also Isaiah 48:1.

37. 2 Nephi 5:15–16.

38. 1 Nephi 19:24.

39. 1 Nephi 19:23.

40. 1 Nephi 20:10.

41. 1 Nephi 21:8.

42. 1 Nephi 21:15–16.

43. Abraham 2:11.

44. 2 Nephi 22:2.

45. Alma 46:40.

46. See Nibley, *Approach to the Book of Mormon*, p. 361.

47. Ibid.

48. Jacob 4:8.

49. Mosiah 4:9.

50. Jacob 7:7.

51. 2 Nephi 9:28.

52. 2 Nephi 28:5.

53. 2 Nephi 28:6.

54. 2 Nephi 28:7.

55. 2 Nephi 28:8.

56. 2 Nephi 28:29.

57. 2 Nephi 29:7–8, 12.

58. 2 Nephi 30:2.

59. 2 Nephi 25:26.

60. 2 Nephi 31:13.

61. 2 Nephi 32:3.

62. 2 Nephi 31:17–18.

63. 2 Nephi 31:19–20.

64. 2 Nephi 33:3.

65. 2 Nephi 33:13, 11.

66. Jacob 1:17.

67. See 2 Nephi 2:4; 11:3.

68. Jacob 4:6.

69. Jacob 1:10.

70. Jacob 1:11.

71. Jacob 2:6.

72. Jacob 2:13.

73. Jacob 2:21.

74. Jacob 2:17.

75. Jacob 2:18.

76. Enos 1:4.

77. Jacob 1:2.

78. Mormon 9:27.

79. Enos 1:3.

80. Enos 1:4–6.

81. Enos 1:1.

82. See also 1 Nephi 1:1–2; Mosiah 1:2.

83. Sorenson, *Ancient American Setting*, pp. 294–95.

84. Omni 1:9.

85. Jarom 1:8.

86. Jarom 1:5.

87. Jarom 1:6.

88. Omni 1:12.

89. Nibley, *Approach to Book of Mormon*, pp. 295–309.

90. Mosiah 2:14, 17.

91. Mosiah 4:5.

92. Mosiah 2:20–21.

93. Mosiah 3:19.

94. Mosiah 3:13.

95. Mosiah 4:5–6.

96. Mosiah 2:24.

97. Mosiah 4:2.

98. Mosiah 5:2.

99. Mosiah 5:7.

100. Omni 1:12.

101. See Mosiah 7:3; Alma 10:2–3; Mormon 1:5.

102. Mosiah 11:27.

103. Mosiah 11:19.

104. Mosiah 11:3.

105. Mosiah 11:11.

106. Mosiah 12:13.

107. Mosiah 12:20–21.

108. Mosiah 12:25.

109. Mosiah 13:28.

110. Mosiah 13:33.

111. Mosiah 13:3.

112. Mosiah 17:15.

113. Mosiah 11:8.

114. Mosiah 11:13.

115. Mosiah 18:7.

116. Mosiah 18:26.

117. Mosiah 18:8–9.

118. Mosiah 18:21.

119. Mosiah 18:30.

120. Mosiah 18:18.

121. See Mosiah 18:35.

122. Joseph L. Allen, *Exploring the Lands of the Book of Mormon* (Orem, Utah: S.A. Publishers, 1989), p. 55.

123. Ether 6:10.

124. Mosiah 22:6.

125. Mosiah 18:34.

126. Mosiah 21:3.

127. Mosiah 21:13.

128. Mosiah 24:9.

129. Mosiah 24:11.

130. Mosiah 24:14.

131. Mosiah 8:1.

132. Ibid.

133. Mosiah 24:13.

134. Mosiah 24:21.

135. Mosiah 24:19.

SECTION 3:

TO SING THE SONG OF REDEEMING LOVE

1. Mosiah 27:9.

2. Mosiah 27:11.

3. Mosiah 27:13.

4. There is a seeming discrepancy between two days and nights or three days and nights between Mosiah

27 and Alma 36, but actually one refers to the total time period; the other refers to the time *after* Alma the younger is brought to his father.

5. Alma 36:12–14.

6. Alma 36:17.

7. Mosiah 27:14.

8. Alma 36:18.

9. Alma 36:20–21.

10. Mosiah 27:35.

11. Mosiah 28:3.

12. Mosiah 28:13.

13. See Ether 3:22–24.

14. Alma 1:27.

15. Alma 1:32.

16. Mosiah 29:26–27.

17. Alma 4:6.

18. Alma 4:9.

19. Alma 4:19.

20. Alma 5:14.

21. Alma 5:26.

22. Alma 8:15.

23. Alma 8:18.

24. Matthew 4:20.

25. Alma 9:4.

26. Alma 11:44.

27. Alma 11:43.

28. Alma 12:14.

29. Alma 13:3.

30. See, for example, *History of the Church*, 6:307.

31. Alma 14:6.

32. Alma 14:10.

33. Alma 15:18.

34. Alma 14:11.

35. Alma 14:26.

36. Alma 14:29.

37. Sorenson, *Ancient American Setting*, p. 295.

38. Alma 17:13.

39. Alma 17:14.

40. Alma 17:17.

41. Hugh Nibley, *The Prophetic Book of Mormon* (Salt Lake City and Provo, Utah: Deseret Book and F.A.R.M.S., 1989), p. 486.

42. Ibid., p. 487.

43. Ibid.

44. Alma 17:20.

45. Nibley, *Approach to the Book of Mormon*, p. 402.

46. D&C 1:38.

47. Alma 18:11.

48. Alma 17:26.

49. Alma 18:24, 32.

50. Alma 18:41.

51. Alma 19:6.

52. Alma 19:16.

53. Alma 19:33.

54. Alma 20:10.

55. Alma 20:23.

56. Alma 22:3.

57. Alma 22:15–16.

58. Alma 22:18; italics added.

59. C. S. Lewis, *Mere Christianity* (New York: Macmillan, 1986), p. 175.

60. Alma 23:6.

61. Alma 26:20.

62. Alma 24:11–13.

63. Alma 24:18.

64. Alma 24:21.

65. Alma 9:4.

66. Alma 27:8.

67. Alma 26:9.

68. Alma 27:17–18.

69. Alma 17:2–3.

70. Alma 26:5.

71. Alma 30:17.

72. Nibley, *Prophetic Book of Mormon*, p. 349.

73. Alma 30:23.

74. Ibid.

75. Alma 30:40.

76. 2 Nephi 26:29.

77. Alma 31:30.

78. Alma 31:16–18.

79. Nibley, *Prophetic Book of Mormon*, p. 344.

80. Alma 31:5.

81. Alma 32:17.

82. Alma 32:28.

83. John 1:1.

84. Alma 32:42; see Galatians 4:19.

85. Alma 31:23.

86. Alma 34:20–26.

87. Alma 34:28.

88. Alma 32:41.

89. Alma 32:42.

90. Alma 5:48.

91. D&C 122:7.

92. Nibley, *Prophetic Book of Mormon*, p. 542.

93. Alma 39:11.

94. Alma 41:10.

95. Alma 39:8.

96. Catherine Thomas, "The Sermon on the Mount," in *Studies in Scripture, Volume 5, The Gospels*, ed. Kent P. Jackson and Robert L. Millet (Salt Lake City: Deseret Book, 1986), pp. 238–39.

97. Alma 41:14–15.

98. Alma 34:34.

99. Alma 39:9.

100. Nibley, Prophetic Book of Mormon, p. 542.

101. Alma 37:23.

102. See pre-1981 editions of the Doctrine and Covenants, sections 78:9; 82:11; 104:26, 43, 45, 46. See also Bruce R. McConkie, *Mormon Doctrine*, rev. ed. (Salt Lake City: Bookcraft, 1966), pp. 307–8.

103. Alma 37:19.

104. *Journal of Discourses*, 19:38.

105. Alma 37:9.

106. Alma 37:45.

107. See F. Richard Hauck, *Deciphering the Geography of the Book of Mormon* (Salt Lake City: Deseret Book, 1988), p. 10.

108. Alma 47:22.

109. Alma 46:12.

110. Alma 46:13.

111. Alma 46:21.

112. Alma 48:11, 17.

113. Alma 43:18.

114. See Alma 43:37.

115. Alma 48:11.

116. See Alma 49:27.

117. See Alma 57:20–21.

118. Alma 53:13.

119. Alma 53:15.

120. Alma 56:39.

121. Alma 56:33, 46.

122. Alma 56:45.

123. Alma 56:44, 47.

124. Hauck, *Deciphering the Geography*, p. 9

125. Alma 56:54.

126. Alma 56:55–56.

127. Alma 57:26.

128. Alma 60:3.

129. Alma 60:5.

130. Alma 60:7.

131. Alma 61:9.

132. Alma 61:17.

133. Alma 53:3–4. See also Alma 50:1–5.

134. Sorenson, *Ancient American Setting*, p. 301.

135. Ezra Taft Benson, *Ensign*, November 1988, p. 87.

136. Helaman 6:21.

137. Helaman 2:9.

138. Helaman 2:13.

139. Ether 8:22, 24.

140. Helaman 4:12.

141. Helaman 4:13.

142. *Journal of Discourses*, 2:176.

143. Helaman 5:23–24.

144. Helaman 5:28.

145. Helaman 5:30.

146. Helaman 5:36.

147. Helaman 5:44.

148. Helaman 5:49.

149. Helaman 6:1.

150. Nibley, *Prophetic Book of Mormon*, p. 474.

151. Ibid., p. 368.

152. Alma 63:4.

153. Helaman 8:14–15.

154. Sorenson, *Ancient American Setting*, p. 99.

155. Mosiah 9:9.

156. Sorenson, *Ancient American Setting*, p. 100.

157. Helaman 8:26.

158. Helaman 8:6.

159. Helaman 12:6.

160. Helaman 8:27.

161. Helaman 9:27.

162. Helaman 9:29.

163. Sorenson, *Ancient American Setting*, p. 158.

164. 1 Nephi 19:7.

165. Helaman 9:31.

166. Helaman 9:33.

167. Helaman 10:4–5.

168. Helaman 11:4.

169. Helaman 12:2–3.

170. Helaman 11:25.

171. Helaman 12:1–2.

172. Helaman 13:25.

173. Helaman 13:22.

174. Helaman 13:18.

175. Helaman 14:2, 4.

176. Helaman 14:6–7.

177. See Sorenson, *Ancient American Setting*, p. 290.

178. See Ether 9:19.

179. See Mosiah 9:9.

SECTION 4:
ARISE AND COME FORTH UNTO ME

1. Helaman 16:18.

2. Helaman 16:20.

3. 3 Nephi 1:6.

4. 3 Nephi 1:7.

5. 3 Nephi 1:9.

6. 3 Nephi 1:13.

7. 3 Nephi 1:15.

8. 3 Nephi 1:17, 19.

9. Zechariah 14:6–7.

10. See 3 Nephi 2:5–8.

11. Alma 30:60.

12. 3 Nephi 2:1.

13. 3 Nephi 2:2.

14. Mormon 9:24; italics added.

15. Exodus 14:12.

16. Mosiah 27:16.

17. Alma 9:9.

18. D&C 45:65.

19. D&C 45:66–67.

20. 3 Nephi 3:2.

21. 3 Nephi 3:3.

22. 3 Nephi 3:4.

23. 3 Nephi 3:5.

24. 3 Nephi 3:9.

25. 3 Nephi 3:8.

26. 3 Nephi 3:15.

27. See Hauck, *Deciphering the Geography*, p. 12.

28. See Alma 52:9; 3 Nephi 3:25.

29. See 3 Nephi 3:23–24.

30. See, for example, Alma 22:32–33.

31. See Alma 22:32. The descriptions given in the Book of Mormon of the narrow neck of land and the narrow pass that led into the land northward so perfectly match this region that it is hard not to recognize this area as being the most probable candidate. Space does not allow the verification of sites fortified not only during the 73 B.C. wars, but also during the last series of battles with General Mormon leading up the narrow neck and into the land northward. Years of tradition have pointed to the Isthmus of Tehuantepec in Mexico as being the narrow neck of land, but on-site observations do not seem to support this unlikely candidate.

32. 3 Nephi 7:18.

33. 3 Nephi 4:7.

34. Ibid.

35. 3 Nephi 5:1.

36. 3 Nephi 6:14.

37. 3 Nephi 6:12.

38. 3 Nephi 8:3.

39. 3 Nephi 8:5.

40. 3 Nephi 8:7.

41. 3 Nephi 8:12.

42. Sorenson, *Ancient American Setting*, p. 321.

43. See Allen, *Exploring the Lands*, p. 231.

44. 3 Nephi 10:9.

45. 3 Nephi 10:14.

46. 3 Nephi 8:20.

47. 3 Nephi 8:21.

48. 3 Nephi 8:23.

49. 3 Nephi 8:24.

50. 3 Nephi 8:25.

51. Joseph Smith–Matthew 1:42.

52. 3 Nephi 9:2, 13, 15.

53. 3 Nephi 10:5–6.

54. 3 Nephi 10:8.

55. 3 Nephi 10:9.

56. 3 Nephi 10:10.

57. 3 Nephi 10:12.

58. 3 Nephi 11:1.

59. 3 Nephi 11:3.

60. 3 Nephi 11:7.

61. 3 Nephi 11:8.

62. 3 Nephi 11:10.

63. Doctrine and Covenants 45:51–52.

64. 2 Nephi 31:15.

65. 2 Nephi 31:11.

66. 2 Nephi 31:20.

67. 3 Nephi 11:11.

68. 3 Nephi 11:12.

69. 3 Nephi 11:14.

70. John 10:27.

71. John 10:14.

72. D&C 50:41.

73. 3 Nephi 11:15.

74. 3 Nephi 11:17.

75. Many of the observations in this caption are based on the careful research of F. Richard Hauck, Ph.D., yet to be published, shared verbally with the authors on site. Dr. Hauck has made incredible discoveries here and throughout Mesoamerica relating to the Book of Mormon.

76. See Allen, *Exploring the Lands*, pp. 159–60.

77. 3 Nephi 11:37.

78. 3 Nephi 14:7.

79. 3 Nephi 12:40.

80. 3 Nephi 13:4.

81. 3 Nephi 13: 25, 27.

82. 3 Nephi 12:5.

83. 3 Nephi 12:7.

84. 3 Nephi 15:17.

85. 3 Nephi 17:1–3.

86. 3 Nephi 17:5.

87. 3 Nephi 17:6–7.

88. 3 Nephi 17:9.

89. 3 Nephi 17:8.

90. 1 Nephi 7:12.

91. 3 Nephi 19:35.

92. 3 Nephi 26:14, 16.

93. 3 Nephi 17:14.

94. Ibid.

95. 3 Nephi 17:15–17.

96. 3 Nephi 27:13.

97. 3 Nephi 17:20.

98. 3 Nephi 17:21, 24.

99. See Moses 7:69.

100. See JST, Genesis 14:33–34.

101. *Journal of Discourses*, 21:94.

102. 3 Nephi 18:7.

103. 3 Nephi 20:8.

104. 3 Nephi 19:2–3.

105. 3 Nephi 19:8.

106. 3 Nephi 19:13.

107. 3 Nephi 19:23.

108. 3 Nephi 19:25.

109. 3 Nephi 16:1.

110. See 2 Nephi 29:12–14.

111. 3 Nephi 26:3.

112. 3 Nephi 26:13.

113. 3 Nephi 26:11, 6–9.

114. 3 Nephi 26:3.

115. 3 Nephi 26:4.

116. 3 Nephi 20:29.

117. 3 Nephi 20:22.

118. 3 Nephi 21:14–18.

119. 3 Nephi 22:17.

120. 3 Nephi 22:10.

121. 3 Nephi 28:1.

122. 1 Nephi 11:2.

123. 3 Nephi 28:2.

124. 3 Nephi 28:5.

125. 3 Nephi 28:8–10.

126. 3 Nephi 28:13.

127. 3 Nephi 28:15.

128. 3 Nephi 28:20.

129. D&C 14:7.

130. 3 Nephi 27:8.

131. 4 Nephi 1:15.

132. 4 Nephi 1:16.

133. 4 Nephi 1:3.

134. 4 Nephi 1:17.

135. Sorenson, *Ancient American Setting*, p. 128.

136. 4 Nephi 1:25.

137. 4 Nephi 1:32–33.

138. Alma 5:54.

139. Mosiah 4:19.

140. 4 Nephi 1:26.

141. 4 Nephi 1:24.

142. 4 Nephi 1:46.

SECTION 5:
O YE FAIR ONES, HOW IS IT THAT YE COULD HAVE FALLEN!

1. Mormon 2:10.

2. Mormon 2:18.

3. Mormon 1:2.

4. Mormon 1:15.

5. See Mormon 1:6.

6. See Mormon 1:15.

7. See Mormon 1:7.

8. Mormon 2:13.

9. Nibley, *Approaching Zion*, p. 17.

10. Mormon 2:15.

11. Mormon 3:12.

12. Moroni 9:6.

13. Mormon 6:4.

14. Ibid.

15. Mormon 5:2.

16. Moroni 9:10.

17. Mormon 5:17–18.

18. Mormon 6:7.

19. Mormon 6:8.

20. Some scholars believe the battle lasted far longer than one day because of the large number slain. In the abridgment, Mormon may have left out details of a long, drawn-out battle.

21. Mormon 6:14.

22. Mormon 6:17.

23. Mormon 1:19.

24. Mormon 6:6.

25. Mormon 8:2.

26. Mormon 8:5.

27. Moroni 1:2–3.

28. Moroni 8:3.

29. Moroni 8:2; 8:9; 9:1; 9:6; 9:11.

30. See Allen, *Exploring the Lands*, p. 20. See also pp. 137–47.

31. Ether 2:8.

32. Ether 15:22.

33. Nibley, *Lehi in the Desert*, p. 245.

34. *History of the Church*, 2:66.

35. Mormon 6:19–20.

36. Mormon 8:35.

37. Mormon 8:31.

38. Mormon 8:36.

39. Ether 12:4.

40. Mormon 9:9.

41. Mormon 9:11.

42. Moroni 7:37.

43. Moroni 7:47.

44. Moroni 7:45.

45. Moroni 10:4–5.

"And now . . . all ye ends of the earth, hearken unto these words and believe in Christ . . .

for they are the words of Christ, and he hath given them unto me;

and they teach all men that they should do good . . . for Christ will show unto you,

with power and great glory, that they are his words, at the last day;

and you and I shall stand face to face before his bar;

and ye shall know that I have been commanded of him to write these things,

notwithstanding my weakness.

And I pray the Father in the name of Christ that many of us, if not all,

may be saved in his kingdom at that great and last day. . . .

I speak unto you as the voice of one crying from the dust:

Farewell until that great day shall come."

The Prophet Nephi, 544 B.C.

2 Nephi 33:10–13